Spellcaster's
Manual

the collected poems of
Ainsley Burrows

BurrowsInk

Introduction

In 1998 I left graduate school one semester into an MBA program. Three days earlier I had survived a car accident in which the car rolled over five times... It should have been fatal, but me and my two friends all walked away from the wreckage without a scratch. On that day I decided I would pursue my true love, writing, for the rest of my life.

This Collection, *The Spellcaster's Manual*, contains the 10 books of poetry that I have written since then. (only the last three have been previously published)

Art & Magic
The Dog Of All Things
Swag Of Scars
Sorcerer's Daughter
Spellcaster's Manual
The Wealth Of Nations
The Book Of Forms
Black Angels With Sky Blue Feathers
The Woman Who Isn't Was
The Wolf Who Cried Boy

Cover Photo: Barron Claiborne
Editor: Laurielle Noel
Assistant Editors: Chantel Langlois & Olivia Stephenson

CONTENTS

BOOK I : Art & Magic

BOOK II : The Dog Of All Things

BOOK III : Swag Of Scars

BOOK IV: Sorcerer's Daughter

BOOK V: Spellcaster's Manual

BOOK VI: The Wealth Of Nations

BOOK VII: The Book Of Forms

BOOK VIII: Black Angels With Sky Blue Feathers

BOOK IX: The Woman Who Isn't Was

BOOK X: The Wolf Who Cried Boy

Book I

ART & MAGIC

(2014-2017)

Of Brooklyn

She walks like a
magnetic cluster of suns
carrying realms
of bronzed antelopes
heart like paradise leaping
rapt in winged sonnets
a song sculpted from
tender stone

she walks
like an earthquake weeping
and those aren't hips
those are secret empires
branches of understanding
defying gravity
stills of thunder rehearsing
paintings of scrambled light

she walks
trailed by the eyes
of a million
light headed fools
fumbling over their tongues
she is made of ten
unbelievable women
squeezed into this
singular heaven
like watched stars
we marvel

she walks
like a new chaos
created from unnamed
instruments
stranger, you
soften the ridges

and the fault lines
we endure
so we gladly
worship
at your shrine.

Trumpian darkness

There is a wolf in the high-rise
speaking in fluent sheep
some capitalist dipped
in the nuclear code
ego the size of a nightmare
a wall marching through his head
he's a failed state
coded in hate
he speaks in swastika

some nativist dog whistle
ranting about immigrants entering
as if America is a
helpless virgin
being ravaged by
some dark savage
smells like the birth of a nation
DW Griffith as a toddler
in a giant red tie

with breath like knives
Klan teeth
alt-right toupee
children coifed
like children of the corn
hoping you forget to remember
he's a blanket cut from treason
tapped phones and bank loans
tapped the psyche of those
allergic to logic

the sacred spaces of women
men who crush the heads
of the less fortunate
small men who see themselves
as your superior
men who will burn the world
to prove they are right
even when the facts say
Mr. Trump you are wrong.

The thoughts of ants

What if we are all
crafted pieces of sky
stars conversing
in total darkness
what if birth is ink
life, a snail
in the faint perfume
of exist

what if to be is to ain't
and ain't ain't even ain't
what if the universe is
god's heart rolled up
into a coil, ticking
and religion
our dreams pierced

what if we are all geniuses
drunk on reality
and the devil is
a bullet
riding side saddle
through the projects

what if insanities
are dream-storms
thought-quakes
or psychic meteor showers

what if truth
is the administered

myth of a billion screaming
stomachs lost in scripture

what if lies
are the administered
myth of a billion screaming
stomachs lost in scripture

oh, how they love us holy
and blind, heaven
rotating about us
transfigured
in the age of shame
solar gradation
statistical skin color
a complex so complex
we suffer from future
dis-disbelief

what if this is one
of a billion universes
and god can't find us
have you seen the night sky
like a battlefield
of zodiac phrasing
yet we dare to think
our thoughts are more
important than the thoughts
of ants

what if we are
computer programs
written by trees
by soil

24

by microscopic beings
and we tumble
like a cosmic blind spot
praying to the republic
of race
of sex
of nation
with our god on a leash
trying to out-control time
trying to dice and stretch
the glistening philosophy
dogma the metaphor
metaphor the truth
truth the myth
myth our fostered fears
used to raise victims
to fill ships
and ovens
and pews
and eras
and campuses
and factories
and streets
to build machines
to expand the bandwidth
of the karma
our children will face
all the smiles manufactured
by empires
stored in emporiums
stadiums full
addicted to outward expansion
afraid of inner
light

so we watch cigarettes
eating rivers
spray cans devouring trees
as our children conquer
artificial armies
murder on play stations
their hands
covered
in Hitler
in nationalist particulars
versed in the art
of preemptive stupidity

what if this is one
of a billion universes
and god can't find us
have you seen the night sky
like a battle field
of zodiac phrasing
yet we dare to think
our thoughts are more
important than the thoughts
of ants.

Brotha seal blue

I am seal blue
teal blue
real blue
blue blue
blue black
black black
too black
ship black
hip black
sick black
dick black
crack black
don't crack
crick crack
wont crack

italist, vitalist
-egan, vegan
herbs verbs
last of the Mohawk

so dark
half black
three fifths Indian
so Bama
Obama
OJ
noose juice
hood good
pimp limp
white lines
so chalk
leg drag
head rag
field slave
real brave

found free
bound free
free free
trap trap
rat trap
rat race
race based
at a snail's pace

move white
true white
white, white
white stripes
star spangled
tied up
dried up
the whole body
oh scotty
beam me up
dream me up
yup, dream me up

auction caution
kept it real
kept it steal
commerce
sunstroke
the son broke
the sun spoke
the son woke
from the dead
the mom broke
in two twice
snake eyes
snake bite
snake rattle
human cattle
twice bitten
twice scrambled

true story
why lie
when we can't die.

Brownsville

A cop carrying
a hip full of
metal nooses
blue
uniform stiff with
conquered streets

a thousand negroid faces
that mock the sun
defy the light
existing beneath
the gavel's echo
historying itself

a brown boy
hair like gunpowder
waiting for matching shells
to burn its trademark
through him
to sanctify his place
his status below deck
to logo his mother's face emotionless
stuffed inside the smell of pine
still on her hands from cleaning
suburban floors
wood from trees
with rope burns

eyes hooded
a three part harmony
same song sung
in the key of orchestrated fear
one to beat the odds
playing dice with her womb
one to walk the beat
survive these animals intact

the other to beat time
any day now
he is already dead

they'll set the streets on fire
for a heart pounded wrong
bullets pointing out
his supposed inferiority
the explosion
the sound struck her
antique face the
way his body French kissed
the sidewalk
fearless
as if he felt sorry for his hunter
all this blood to clean
her hands
the smell of pine

but who to wipe
the weight from her heart
the grimace from her jaw clenched
to kiss her something terrible
and say, "see you in a few maa."

Haunted house in heels

Is it candle wax
or is it notion
that you want
you, a sycamore
opened by a blade of ice
can you remember
how I whispered
verses of the Apocrypha
into the sacrifice
you presented
a tongue to divine
all the soundless pleasures
licked honeyed heaven
from the fore
of your cup
a mouth full of breasts
alcohol woven
into a trembling grunt
a language so beautiful
it can only be hallucinated
praying to the god of dark
crawled into
your night-soil
stirred the edges
like squandered madness
rose apocalyptic
and fell into your grace
men have always fallen
for guillotines
burning cities
pyres
tempests
tornadoes
and dangerous women
with bosoms filled with infidelity
who are chattering mad

with watchful hair
who wrestle
and gossip
their way through ways
women who dream
of wearing pitch forks
and thundering moans
something about
watching a bird burn
that lights our hearts
that stubborn lump of clay
curiosity like a
slave with wings
we yearn for the
vicious fragrances you
unleash inside us.

Come inside

She presents the door
smiles the way
he cups the entrance
slips her fingers over the knob
turns slowly
her fist clenched
he pushes in
a sigh, a muted
something
meaningless
to the ocean
of onlookers
he goes in behind her
there is water at the door
her feet are wet
he slips as he enters
she has a fist full of
his scent
he exits
wipes his feet
and re-enters
this time
with much care.

Yes he is

God is a room
full of pillows
a waterfall with a Mohawk
a lightning bolt wearing Corinth
God is gas fires and straw hats
electric blindfolds
and jigsaw purple

God is escape clause
and profit
a prophet
a gun runner
a Japanese Christ in Hiroshima
waiting for the bomb
God is the bomb
God is a desert with a tooth ache
the valley of square trees
the story that murdered
the big bang
bang

God is bang and Bible
fear and dread
God is silence in the weeds with
the dark ages between his teeth

God is a pregnancy test
a sky so blue it broke your heart
God broke your heart
God is a bouquet of flowers
God fell in love with the tragedy
trapped in Charlie Chaplin's mustache
God is a circle looking for meaning
a square looking for meaning
God does not give a fuck about meaning

God is cute in shades
she got a fat ass
and a sweet pair of knockers
and she will fuck you for smokes
God will fuck you for smokes
somewhere in Brooklyn
or Shanghai at a bar
having a beer or
a glass of wine
with a whale in it

God just burped
God needs help with his wheelchair
God is wheelchair and
armpits and strobe lights
God is elephants and silk
routes, Slave trade
and balance sheets

God just got kicked, fucked
splayed, sucked
God is ugly and beautiful
and vapid and deep

but most of all
God is silly.

Good god

Imagine god
with Jheri curl
activator dripping
on his new metallic blue suit
shoes a fraction too small
hands ashy
late for work
sweating
forgot his deodorant
squeezed between
a white woman
who is mostly nose
and a wall street
deck of cards
all starch and
teeth, the train jolts
god farts, by accident
a bead of sweat
caresses his neck and slides
under his Adam's apple
he looks at the woman
with disgust
scrunches his face
and says,
"what the fuck?"

Ms. Love

She loves hard
slingshots
her entire body
into love

she craves the crash
the terrifying feeling
of being splintered
but her heart
is made from silicone
so she loves even harder
the next time around

one day she asked me
is it possible to die
from a broken heart?
I said, I did not know
she said, I hope so.

Sanity going once, going twice

There is a place
where
the masses are
content in their
gentle waltz
a mambo even
a tango of mostly

but nothing beats
the truly free
the insane untainted those
who have not been
tricked into sanity
they walk amongst us
speaking to flowers
dancing through cars
with butterfly ears
and sailing saucer eyes
dressed in white or
too much dirt

he, he needs a dollar
to save the sun
got pockets full
of volcanic childhood
screaming at a see-through wall

she needs something to eat
got a slave ship
a cotton field
a lunch counter
if one subdivides the psyche
does each side
play different music

truer still is

the moment we
decided sanity was
more important than freedom
we walked into this
tiny room of world
washed our faces
in the narrow
confines of a
spineless future
and said yes this
this will be my
resting place.

In da club

That body
flesh without
conscience
rolling around
the sound
pounding
fabric arms of smoke
waistline like
evolved syrup
liquid silver on fire

simple
beneath the lights
flashes of thigh
and wrist, ass flesh
and dynamite
sweat like preached heat,
heat smeared delicious
she moves outside
the conventions of reason

of the ogling ignorant
brainless clay figures
their desires like
treacherous drinks
swallowed
spilling from their
stratified trousers
stiff
without heritage
or sense of being
they grasp at straws
while bales of hay
burn inside her loins

she moves like a question

deep at first
then Africa calls it back
cosmics it so
tilts then ignites
a brutal cacophony
of hip gyrations
deliberate
with emphasis on
necessary
dark girl
in a jar of eyes
surrendering to all the given
intangible facts
this is divinity reconciled
unbelievable
and oh
to lick her sweat
from the floor
would be a certain
heaven.

City of dreams

New York
with all its
overpriced cages
nice shiny prisons
of intellect
the sky brandished
over kneeling serfs
we, fattened by
the fat of speed
our lives in a perpetual
whir, the engines
buzzing below
dark steel grinding
into the future
stamping out shipwrecks
and addicts
more and more
meaningless personalities
marching bars full of
new billboards searching
for a newer version
of the newest fool
idiot's apocalypse
skeletons with their
bulimic dreams
they dream of bones
and emptiness
but only the dead or
those drained of eyes
will sit in the stampede of neon
signs that blind our
ambitions to human
our ambitions were
as it may
piles and piles of daydreaming
in skinny jeans so tight

we can only half exist
bleed for the coffers
we resurrect in show houses
on the roof of the hyper-marketed
sits the sanity of
a great age
drunk off belief
the booze in his beard
smelling like the
silence we need
the rumble, the traffic
fogging our senses
our anchored proof
proven wrong
daily chaos stenciled
across the faces of
the young
the unborn with their
new plastique futures
designed by Prada

the Bowery once had meaning
so did the Stuy
truth is
pigs love uniforms
they can pretend
to be horses, with mocked up
beliefs
they protect the punctuated
the north
where the animals
like their teeth
in season
perfect and straight
like nothing else
in the universe
little pieces
of beauty agreed upon
vodka mixed with

shark blood
is all the rave
nude girls
who look like nude boys
the irony of irony
is perpetually ironic
the laughed at
seldom knows
the reason for teeth

without bread
there is no heaven
just darkness and blades
and contracts with fear
there is a district
in the Bronx where
the language is older
the cages outdated
packed with dreamers
clamped to iPods
agreeing to everything
they consume, fabricated
versions of the theory
of who they are
because
the real human is too
heavy to carry
too afraid of love
too permanent
so they set
their minds a dreaming
hoping they too
can be inhaled by
the neon lights.

Heartbreaks

Heartbreaks are
harpoons falling
from heaven
the holiest of places
slamming through
a device so tender
so specific it
translates stimuli
to tears

heartbreaks
are frozen oceans
exploding at sunrise
splashing its
long-legged
emptiness like
celestial daggers
across the what of
what we are

heartbreaks
are chemical equations
dreaming of the flesh
that transmutes
the inner terror
and softens
the mathematical
subtlety of
all our fears

heartbreaks
are proof
that at some
moment prior
we had to have
totally

surrendered
who we are
to another being.

Art & magic

There are places
where prophets walk
where saints and saints alike
gather for the business
the art of undoing
the chaos
where men birth worlds
and women resurrect
light structures
of love and hope
where we pray with
poem and song
with ink and sound
with move and silence
when the alchemy
the magic
the belief
are all bounded up
as one
in small rooms
we gather in the dark
amongst the bright light
and surgeon smiles
ritual our messages
bleeding the scars
of language
divots of genius dug
into our faces
unexplainable sources
of a sorcery we can't explain
can't help but is

there are places
where our loneliness
reside because we are
the misunderstood few

we who walked
into the ocean
saying prayers
ascended into the sky
engulfed in centuries
of established suffering

there are those among us
who believe in everything
and nothing
without ever believing
we know
we know, we know
that we are from realms
of creativity
from corners of
the cosmos where
art is bread
and love is an atom
enchanted by its own
misunderstanding
we live because
live is all
we bloom and inspire
and fall in love with awe
we reel and search
for the simple
in hopes of finding
something beautiful
something to crack us open.

Yes

She teases
not knowing
he saw her
writing a poem
with her tongue
with a half-smile
a smirk
a clever
look in her eye
as if to say
I can do things to you

he saw it
her language
folded neatly
on the page
against her
heaving chest
her movements
mostly
wrist and fingers
and intense wanting
skin flushed with
warm blood
lips like bitten
cherry stems
desire, never this
close for touch
might be dangerous

she walks away with
her smirk
her smile
her cunning
her violin solo
knowing

she could have broken
the dance floor open
dip her organs in
could have
tasted the warm summer
morning brimming with
new life
and the world
would still
rotate in a perfected
kind of beautiful.

Be you

You mimic Jimi
you ain't know where Jimi's been
you ain't never seen
the gashes in his toenails
Vietnam scrawled
all over his guitar
all his friends shipped back in
tiny pieces

Lucifer with napalm
on his breath
and iron in his vocals
that wasn't rage
that was Jimi
you don't wanna be Jimi
you want Jimi's fame

you don't want
the blackness
he deserved or
the needle exploding
in your face
serpents crawling out
your arms
teeth like burning flags
whores for breakfast
blood for lunch
a mistake so brutal
all the heroin couldn't cure
the smile he lost
in a photo

yet you wanna be Jimi
not when he married a hacksaw
to his shin
set his liver on fire

then
brought it on stage
the newly visible
always finds it hard
in the world of the visibles
trying to out-live
their expiration date
you, you don't want
to be Jimi.

Music

Fuck the violin
I'd rather watch you lick
the music from the bow
approach you from behind
levitate that mini skirt
spread your pages
and climb into your g-spot
watch you gyrate
sticky sheets of music
from your pulsing core
then lick the juices from the
conductors baton

the truth is
I am only trying
to sample your bassline
leave teeth marks on the blue black
split your spine wide open
to analyze your ride position
call me Dr. Break-back-anosis
maybe we could aria and crescendo
slow down time
watch your moans gather then explode
into erratic brush strokes

you could Dali me
I could Basquiat you
like a voodoo ritual
like some sweaty hedonistic
orgy, our organs calling out for
Jesus, like you ain't know
I was a sorcerer
invite your girls
you'll wake up in
moon boots and eye patches
like you didn't know I was midnight

carrying handcuffs
conjuring orgasms out of thin air

you could be Bible study
I'll be the sermon
we could set our hearts on fire
and move to the sound
of the wood smacking
against the timpani
music slowly
pushed into supple flesh
the sap spilling
splashed symphonic all over your lap
like a guitar rift in heat
the edges pushed all the way back
the juices, the chords
sliding over our knuckles

I'm on bass and you're on keys
and the tempo is building
and the humidity is topless
nipples singing hallelujah
I'm behind this sexy
dark bodied upright
pressed against my pelvis
the notes building
the neck of the bass
slippery with sweat
the hefty hypotenuse ripe
and throbbing

I'm plucking
and you're hitting them
high note and changing the key
and the tempo
the secret religion gyrating
bodies speaking
the bass, the keys
organs weeping

almost to the point of insanity
muscles tighten
this is the ecstasy of
sweet darkness
your lips slightly open
I can taste you like a
metaphor extracted
from sprawled soil.

Garvey

We remember you
wrapped in
red
black
green
voice like a
beautiful ball of fire.

Sammy Sosa

Dear Sammy
it is your eyes
you at home-plate all squint
all the billion cells of you
hunched over
swinging
that club
that metal pipe
to send your challenge
to high heaven
you, a beautiful midnight
filled with perfect timing
those eyes Sammy
that kept you in contact
with the ball
says more than
I can decode

you seem so happy Sammy
now that you can afford
to buy your way, to freedom
no, now that you can renovate
out of your shackle of skin
those teeth Sammy
I remember them checked
you at the plate
they can't lie
that grin says
I am finally free
of this canopy of dark skin
hair like a new silk dress
all that heritage carried
with such nobility
it broke my heart
to see you bleached eons
pushed overboard

drowning in the total blue

Sammy
did you pray
to the gods of pain
to eat this blackness away?
how many times did Disney
run the commercial before you knew
for sure that
this body was a curse,
Sammy?

Don't be mad

You gave him your womb
overwhelmed
by the pilgrimage
your kingdom conquered
named him god
dreamed up a past life
surrounded by tents
arms craving
you gave him your womb
now you protest
deity of powdered forms
glorified soulmate
dislodged

this bleeding is
your own choosing
you cried
because
the concrete is setting
this bleeding
named him god
gave him your womb
legs spread powerless
offered him feathers
plumes and the core
of woven darkness
could have been love
yes
but on the first night
maybe lust
illuminated by sweet
stumbling caramel liquor
the appetite
tossing clothes
a flock of golden priest
centuries old

heads like
antique lamps
begged you to turn, but
no, you bit into the fruit
now your heart is suspended
between the
oracle and the stone
the ultimate jigsaw
you handed him
your skirt folded
your locked box
of treasures
now you blame him for
the deciphered fragments
he left on your sheets.

Children of the night sky

Tributaries fanned out
across the land
a trampled people
religion for knives
corpses for wealth
a funeral of torches
a klan of night walkers
horses clashed up against
their squandered equality
the small laughter-hushed

stories of midnight
swinging moons on fire
wailing contortions
of the royal amputee
earth bound memoirs
to feed the lawn
a raged humiliation
the women carry
their eyes like
failed trinkets

the tide turns
and the sun still
hangs low, pierced
with metal frustration
poverty of night siren
ushered steel to explode
to disease the teeth
to scalp the lung
to dwell them
permanent in merciless
towers of intoxication
of never remembering, yet

they grow immune

to the new blindness
they see beyond the visible
spectrum
they stretch
and create gods
and myths
on rooftops
they take to the sky
their crowned hearts
insisting on the greatest
of prophecies
heads pregnant
with exploding spheres
and impossible songs
these dark symbols
dreaming from the center
of cells
exiled within the self
unembarrassed by the
roots sprouted
they from
they fly and dream
beautiful dreams.

Secret of dance

Dancers know
the absolute ecstasy
the fire, the chaos of
vigilant drums
pouring footsteps
from the body

silos filled with songs
sleeping among the bones
build me a temple
of perspired clarity
fatigue like a grounded anthem
arguing with muscle
the lines
the flesh, legs like notes of music
brushed by twilight
bodies flung in silent wonder
trance like
trance like processions
communal nakedness
their stories move
shoulders
wrists
hands circling hips
heaven paused
seven halos erupting
casting spells
this is the original orbit
the original scattering
a ritual of release.

Crude oil

There are pipelines
from Alaska to Washington
from the Black Sea
to the Indian Ocean
pipelines that move
raw material into the hurried
bellies of the capital gods

there are pipelines
that traffic liquid
currency into homes
water to civilize, to clean
pipelines deliver
out of full view
they work night and day
to make sure pockets
are papered or coined
that black crude is moved
from inner earth
to oil the wheels of industry

there are pipelines
in Brooklyn
invisible tubes plugged
into elementary school
classes
pipes that run directly
under Breevort projects
that traffic 8 year old boys
into an industry so
complex
prison is simple
legal slavery tendered
to grease the palms
of suburbanites
poverty is the new oil field

black boys are crude, oiled,
barreled and shipped
fostered
cared for, taken care of
special editions
to be detained in juvenile
detention
the history books will say
his mama was a firearm
his sister was a crack rock
he got caught with his family
down, around his ankles
courted by the
constitution
and maybe it's just that his skin
reminds the judge of oil
nine year old adult
convicted for breathing

he lives in the streets
and oil spills can't speak
put your hands over your head
homeless
no
he is an island boy
Rikers Island
is the new oil rig
in the middle of the ocean
pipelines
they work night and day
to make sure pockets
are papered or coined
that black crude is moved
from inner city
to oil the wheels of industry.

New animals

Orange
wings like mighty
swaths of cloth
an animal imagined
contained only by grace
moves like an abstraction across
the blue endless overworld
changes directions like
a liquid swan of the sky
the mercury of future transport
a lab experiment
a cross between
horse and ballerina
goldfish and eagle
fins and wings and tentacles
for landing, to hover
organic
space craft of flesh
song and science
your flight
orchestrated
in the infinite randomness
of a leaf falling.

Dig

Give me listening things
spirit and curious eyes
a prostitute with a mouth
full of butterflies
a mother of facts with rain
mist and slippery

give me powerful conjuring
writhing alternate universe
drunk on love
and exploration
cries like the twice silent
bottomless sellers
of the night
hips to call you god
scars to history us

give me dark
the fleshy paradox
sticky with reason
the carnival spread
storm-like
for the heart to believe
in firewood and fragrant
sex tightening noise
to kiss you two sunsets
of perfected redemption

watch you drip into
the love spot
vibrate until oily
brilliant colors
come exploding
from our loins.

And god

Beaten iron
sculpted by flames
choked until instruments
appear, instruments
to make sounds
to open the body

the machine gun is
sister to syringe
a mechanism
to abort your sons
with bullets

babies armed with news briefs
corporate breast milk
to cure the pain
to spin the spin
cult-like believers
from Bismarck to Bush

there is a monk
in Cambodia
dosed in gasoline
meditating in perfect French
there is a twelve year old boy
in Israel praying to a tank
his identical twin is Palestinian
with grenade for teeth

there is a boy in Kansas
his head a swastika of flesh
he prays for the death
of night
a young woman in Brooklyn
as dark as Mississippi
bleached to oblivion

eyes like Montana
she believes in Elle

we all believe because
it bring us closer to divinity
away from the empty
gives us glimpses of
the frantic dialogue between
the stars and the soil.

Book II

THE DOG OF ALL THINGS

(2013-2014)

Child-hood

The smell of cane
leaves me nostalgic
humid flashes of childhood
children racing through
streams, their combined
features
landscaped
continents shoved together
arms like blades of
elephant grass

human aero planes flying
filled with songs, darting
bare footed
into an open field
their feet
lift them dirge-like
above the branches
their bodies mourn
in the evening light
like narratives of
multiple sleep

the smell of cane
calls up from history
escapes me this place
of celebrated hunters
curators of riffle fire
concubines of suspicion
thunder carriers
coughing cinders
obtuse in the skin fear

the children on my block they
they do not know
the smell of cane

the feel of feet on grass

what happened to
the empires of children
their spontaneous initiations
into secret worlds
they jabbered into being

where is the space for these
discoverers of timelessness
these astronomers of
converging dreams
they who could translate
the language of flowers
into the language of whales
these daughters and sons
of perpetual play

what happened to
all the moons they invented
the robots they took
through dimensions
the sunshine they prayed for
the happiness
they so loved.

John *(for John Muhammad: The DC Sniper)*

Lethal injection
did not kill you John
you died the day
you enlisted, agreed
to murder strangers
for a country you loved
in a land you barely knew

the sand
came back in your shoes
the kill-switch failed
left you Judas still
your watchful eye still
yearning for the heat
the race of blood
the explosion
the smell of burnt powder
barreling through the
apparatus that binds you
in the jaws of a country
conditioned
against women
and the sons they provide

what was the last
love song you memorized
John before
they escorted you
through that gregarious pageantry
of organized murder
how did they convince you
did they twist your arm
your psyche
what proof did they concoct
spooned
into your head, your veins

what mathematical theorem
imparted they - to equate
human
to enemy
to heartbreak
lost love
and destruction

when did the maps morph
when did
Iraq become DC
patriot
love
country
enemy
soldier
the flesh is not target
not enemy
your son John, remember
the million Muhammads
we murdered
for country
and love
the planes whistling by
the hospital
the pills like cities from above
the pain impossible to shake

John
father of four
what of your children?
when they ask after you
who will quote the day you enlisted
mostly, I think they will say
you were a monster
a murderer-self-taught
a murderer of strangers
a terrorist

John Muhammad
killed Tuesday
at 9:11pm
the day before
Veterans day.

America

I'm a 75 year old man
you are a 7 year old child
yet, you chose to call me
boy.

Love 1784

Let's lay atop this pyre
with glorious smiles
pray our ashes
find the corridors
of their pious hearts
let's rejoice
in that plant food
kind of way
the way our ancestors did
some walked into the ocean
every movement
a natural monologue
strolling down the
boulevard of blood
with talisman in hand
atop this pyre
for it is hard to oppress
bones licked by flames
difficult to exploit
flesh with the soul
exhumed

woman
let's castle
outside all theories
wait there for me
in the cool clearing
with the smell of fever-grass
inside your nostrils
for dawn is impossible
to replace
our instincts
a burnt offering
curled around
the paradise
in your chest

leave me naked, atop
the stairs, heart on fire
roll me into the river of
your tender collapse
watch me apocalypse
inside of you
my breath renamed
let's come back as each other
statues even
with vision colonized
by bronze
I'll feel my way
along every wall
until I find you

woman
lay with me
atop this bale of
warm fluffy whiteness
our palms
smelling like earth
and each other
in violent protest
smiling at the sky
searching for our home
amongst the stampede
of stars
for we have chosen
to shout them down
with our silence
to be beautiful in the house
squandered ugly
we could walk to the moon
you know
the whip singing
like a battalion of knives
and in our anguish
let's pray
for matching tomb stones

their voices inebriated
the smell of fear
like blood hounds
beneath the poplar
the sting
of extracted manhood
thumbs, toes
the tearing into
flesh pulped over
pain like song
hemlock
sycamore
pine
cedar
spinning
rope like grape vine
wine for the ladies
polite in their
ironed exteriors
oblivion tightening
and it's you
I'm thinking of
you
the tips of your fingers
like notes of music
in a field of hay
on our backs
looking up at the stars
choosing a place to meet next.

It doesn't rain

She puts on the wrong face
blond eyes for good measure
the sun is too serious
men
dressed
like orgasms
to soothe the ache

if her
16 year old self
could read the letter
she has become
could see her
inconsistent
like an attic cut in two
all that beautiful brown
hidden behind
decades of caked hatred

she, the harvest
blowing through the streets
searching for someone
to sing love into
this dark shell
she inherited
to ink all the stress away
maybe her first love
possibly
to un-tell her she was ugly

at eight, words
last an infinity
she lost her divinity
defined by another
she loved
too much

waiting for love
the jolly fat man
the chimney's been closed
for 54 years
yet she is keeping vigil
drunk off the contact lenses
she sees the world
disconnected
post identity
for her
it is easier
to be someone else
and loved
than to be herself
and hated, called ugly

so she is in the street
with her blond eyes
to make up for what was
taken.

Good hair

She is four years old
with a million
mega ton volcano
roaring through
her head
subtext, medusa
mother of broken mirrors
surrounded by
a thousand statues
they say you ugly

she is four years old
Indian in a bottle
the genius of the sale
from religious rite
to rite of passage
blame Liz Taylor for playing
Cleopatra
da Vinci for giving
Christ a perm
blame Kizzie
for transporting that gene
kinked in on itself

she is four years old
creamy fire
to fiction her beautiful
if only for a short time
maybe the sting
is a memoir
a flashback
so powerful
it could leave her bald
make her a monk
like the women in India
who donated their hair

sacrificed vanity
she sacrifices for the same
and we all meet, somewhere
in the Indian or the Atlantic
Ocean

she is four years old
the wind blowing gently
through your hair.

Ruin

What of the fragrance
of your beauty?
invisible brush strokes
you religion of canvas
the intensity of your
realized wings
the journey of your halo
eyes to tranquilized god
face like the devil's spell
exiled in the smile's confession
bewitcher of a
thousand stories
ghost of cupid's
smear campaign
the politics of love
is but a bleeding
song for a sorcerer's
ruin.

Red heeled stiletto

Eyes of emerald
limbs like ancient
drawings
body like
remembered silk
heart like a
catastrophic twilight waiting
a chest filled
with splintered cannibals
teeth sharpened
metal smile
a mind to devour, eat
then photograph
your bones

she will gently
stain your flesh
with bitter herbs
marinate in melodies
she has stolen
out of strangers
until you
disintegrate
into sleep
administered
through the tumbled
silences, the crucial parts
of physical night
to then
pull you into
a centuries worth
of proven
aerodynamics.

Stormy weather

His head
filled with dreams
an old city sitting
on an even older bay
carrying a tornado
he yearns in pictures
and light shows
he runs
into the midnight sun
calling out
to the gods we made

he is almost god
a tiny boy
with a microphone
for pockets
who dreams of father
we all do, mother also
both diviners
how about a pound of flesh
nearest the heart
in a language currently
unnoticed

a kingdom for a tweet
an answered call
he is calling
I am calling through
the storm
to a father I barely know
the water splashed
onto his face
a son who doesn't know
me

I have become

my father's heart
the pound of flesh
my mother
made
a monster
raised in a house
free of photos
strange how we occupy
the same heart
same lungs
same voice
yet strangers
to protect and hurt

in all the madness
all the trees fall
storms have no preferences.

Iron heart

He thought her silly
she thought him
a fool
they both smiled
at her life, sad
how she had inherited
this small galaxy

her father
had invented water
she drove
to keep her mind still
life was too short
for seat belts
for sleep
for possessions
for attachments
she was a rogue
of the darker hour
whored herself until
dawn crept in
or until she was too drunk
to die

she never died
just ran into walls
and men
and shredded cities
glass by glass
blame it on the tumor
the size of her childhood
blame it on the water maker
on the sun that melts ice
she writes short notes
to herself

remember to return
this fiction to its owner.

Artists

We are
the bringers of morning
a mountain perched on a bird
we are
music at dawn
a waterfall in ecstasy
a clock wearing dreams
with blinders
poems of eternity burning
a thousand
stars for ransom
we don't exist often
we own the self of self
two galaxies and a paper cup
we love the power of thought
the way heaven moves
we are tomorrow in bifocals
twenty five skies
love incarnate
pieces of November
not for nothing
more after than
moonlight and myth
a heartbeat stumbling
a song of embers
we believe
in stars and ants
ancestors we be
now always
a moment in our breath
we belief in love
and fear and sound
and all things monster
and animal
and beautiful.

Good god damn

Tell her
I'll marry her sweat
under the strobe lights
I'll bend, yes
quiver, maybe
to be that close
to smell her enrapture
all that music
just pumping
into her
the way she
takes it to the floor
shames the devil
but tell her...

Icarus

I carried the sun
it ate a hole through
my spine

burnt a map
onto my palms
head of flames and smoke
I could smell it
Jupiter-like
waiting in my breast pocket
all the forgotten
mediocrats

I carried the sun
on my back
across the sky
like a turtle carrying
an empire
horses galloping
in reverse
their clacking hooves
sucking the sound
back into themselves

as we all slowly
un-fall in love
I carried the sun
until I was all spine
and ash-flesh and
eyes filled with flames.

Morning glory

Sight
is doorway
to belief
born of all the
standardized blue skies
woven like heaven
in labor
the remedy
optioned

the heart
a ball of cloves
the scent of lilac
floating like a gigantic
garden on the current
the aspect overstressed
how many eyes
does it take to see truth
hands to hold up a promise
tears to bury our lost way
how many futures
to explain this pain
parables to fall in love
why we walk
why we pray to sky
that have the same questions
we have

time, with her heart
pressed against
the exposed brick
rib cage catching
the static gallop
like beautiful sirens
to light the dawn
pull daylight out of

our spleen
then braid them into
her flesh, the veins
gently needled
every stitch an imploded
belief system
every suture a nightmare
on layaway

waiting in the coagulated
silence, with a brass empire
hanging from his gun belt
the twinkle, like only
the twinkle could
something soft
antique-like
something Jezebel would
love
without her the empire
does not language
does not prose
simply sits and rots.

Crooner

Saw him
wrapped her in chords
dipped her in a sticky melody
swallowed her whole
her stems in his beard
spat out her sexy bones
italics-like
fingered her
hummed her
guitared her gathered pieces
soaking wet and trembling
caught the shivers
in the back lung

rolled his tongue around
her soft spot, tender
in the throat bedding
covered in blue
Aphrodite with the
charcoal under her nails
the blood grip
stroke
all branch and rope
vocals sweet with perspire
covered in stinky musk
slippery veins
and darling fingers
deep in the wet wet
dark dangerous
chords assembled, regaled
in heaping heat
and rolling hips
to tease leased dreams
make them swampy
increase the liquid throbbing

be it bourbon or moon
all that country boy swag
and twang
to make her irrational
to get all up
in her corner pocket
swindle her thighs
smack her ass type dirty
and tongue her brain
the honey sliding into
her inner ear
his fingers
stroking the guitar
she is with him
deep inside her
where he wants to be
she is on the edge
of her seat
her breath like
oyster's flesh.

I am

I am
two glasses of god
holding hands
looking at the moon
time and motion
mixed with meaning
and a song about love and
a billion other things.

K K K

Your uniforms
are beautiful
fabric like a silk
garden
hanging reds
the whites
blowing ship-like
thru the dark night
torches
your eyes are
a magnificent blue
don't hide those eyes
the history clotted
beneath that hood
is peculiar
twisted
the thirteen stars
twisted
some African mythology
twisted
lost patriots
the rope
god loves
you more than
all the collected niggers
combined
confederates giving
birth to a nation of
blood covered nooses
the horses on fire
screaming racial epithets

I love your commitment
love your human failings
gifted us burning crosses
so we could love you more

burning churches
symbols of a shared god
how lonely you must be
in your superiority
a billion dollar industry
of pain and death
of multiple Mississippi
murders, imported
Darwinist Bible
your desired wife
on some Catholic lap
some Jew sodomizing
your milk white daughter
your ignorance crudely
harnessed to an illusion
so ruthless
moving heaven
could barely
change you.

Out out out

All the way out
in the middle
of Lake Ontario
there is a stretch of water
with a thousand glistening chairs
when the sun retires
below the horizon
and the water is like a sheet
of orange-purple glass
you can almost see
the wind and thoughts
waltzing.

Lady Macbeth

Dear Lady Macbeth
so many think
t'was the blood that forged
your night toil
insane asylum
of empty womb
tomb head
the cancer of
the back story
to maintain
to water daily
the fruits grow
but the plants lie
the two or three people
you were at once
eventually
they will show up at the same opera
no one to sing your praise
to suck compliments from
to feed your low esteem
why is your night so moving
why is you knight moving
face painted with
the lie you are forced
to carry
to repeat
echoes often believe
other echoes...
follow their path
until you believe
this was the destiny

you smeared Duncan's
blood on the dressing room floor
wise old man
hid his eyes

saw you coming
you, a dagger whispered
into your husband cultured hands
a conspiracy to dethrone
he loved you as best he could
to bleed him and then lie
to yourself

lady, did you not
know the price of murder
always splashes
covers more
land than the
concocted stories
you use to soothe the
splintered head
what of the plants
and the sunshine
and the fruits
I hope you nurture them
with water my dear
never blood.

Oh

He imagined
the taste of her lips
woke up in a tub of her fingerprints
and the soft stencil
of her nose
penning the word
"love"
onto his pelvic bone.

Earth mother

Sisters of
the life sigh
visions abundant
possessed lovers
from the corners
of millenniums comes, you
daughters of the sky
talking smack

sharp against the sinews
of the subsidized geography
of over loving
loving like god owes you
a heart filled with beautiful
cycles to change
the blood
monthly pheromoned you
this bleeding
your head the clearinghouse
with scales to balance

zen you be
to lick daylight from
the thoroughfare
pray the womb be still
hope the blood knows
or remembers
the silent hour
when eons were only
moments.

Sports star

Gladiator
adored disposable
famed slave
engine of commerce
capitalism's bitch
inspirer and distraction
sweat like oil prices
they paid for you
designate god monster
kiosk wife
with pearly whites
perpetually
obligated
shareholders
animal instincts and
ballerina toes
million dollar dime
Lincoln
continental
Louisiana
purchased
bought
sold
traded
farmed
minored
leagued
national treasure
a plantation making a deal
Lazarus raising Christ
holy warrior
you are god carrying a
stadium of ropes
and fires
swindled
sold

beneath the ship
loins lobbied
as long as you produce
more versions of
synthesized
murder
branded
numbered
this is
no game.

An exclusive eternity

A man hammers
he is wearing firewood
undergarments
of wordless fevers
parables his way into panties
into the spacious villages of women

their husband's blood
licked from their lips
he will feed her this ape
hand her the medal
besides
a stream runs
through his cage
hands painted
behind his back
she's been fasting
he is skilled at opening
pomegranates
skilled at the circumstances
of gardening

so with all her curiosity
he will fuck her a new kingdom
until she is spare parts
and lovely stranger
abandoned
in a field of hay
the smell of kerosene
in her hair
an unpleasant straw

his mother's hands
smell like charred wood
like an empire of acidic hymns
belligerent in the moonlight

a sickroom
a whore house
his place
her heart harnessed
to a stick of dynamite
resentment
an exclusive eternity

she
loves being pounded
the weight of life
splashed all over her ruthless crotch
disgust
she hates him
he fucks like father
locksmith hands
covered in her childhood
provides
guilt and threshold
she will animal him
call him dog, mongrel
motherfucker
both father, son and holy
for tearing the hinges
off her double door
to easy his dreams
to sucks segments of lying
from his cock
abandoned
in a field of hay

the smell of kerosene
in his hair,
an unpleasant straw
her father's hands
smell like charred wood
like an empire of caustic hymns
belligerent in the moonlight
a sickroom

a whore house
her place
his heart harnessed
to a stick of dynamite
resentment
an exclusive eternity.

For George

George Clinton
dressed up as an alien clone
slave ship dripping
from his beard
martian orisha
sledge hammer
through Beethoven's fifth
funky stone funk
sloppy pink spandex
his heart a bass drum
weed smoke eyes drowning
in a rift, fuck grits
he had a bucket of
runaway foot blisters
distorted maggot-head
kick like a funeral
on heroin
blue veining it
to the star baby
cosmic stink
we all black baby
all blue
all masterpiece
and genius.

Daggers

It was Sunday 2006
super bowl
reggae retro
on Fulton
a few days short of
your appointment with
the butchers
"womb removal"
"no children for me"
"never wanted them anyway"
you said
crazy talk
I buzzed
how silly
to be 29
and womb-less
you made the butcher's case
a case as old as Nigeria
I felt a close relative of shame
you wanted to steal the sun
I just wanted to give you a quiet place
to love you the way
you should love you
lets go to Alaska
you wanted
none of the stars
crumpled
vulnerable
showed you my scars
we traded secrets

I put away my daggers
you hid your fangs
we were friends
on Fulton holding hands
like it was 1970

remember
you kissed me first
wanted to steal the sun
I just wanted to give you a quiet place
to heal
introduce you to the magicians
I knew

she un-spelled you
like a letter through
the night
across the Atlantic
in search of gold
a kingdom
a promise
you didn't care about the
romance of Europe
wrote long letters
like a crazed woman
I can still hear you
tapping in the dark
came back to a Brooklyn
stumbling through mercury
the smell of flint
and Peoria in the air
no joke

we went to your camp
the guards were armed
you cut me to pieces
called it self-defense
I walked away, your claws
dripping the stories
of my mother leaving
you too
you too
I showed you my scars
showed you my scars
we traded secrets

I put away my daggers
you hid your fangs
we were friends
on Fulton holding hands
like it was 1970
remember

your confederates carried
my casket
left it at the wrong door
at the wrong city gate
you put another sword in
then set me on fire
my dreams were burning
you kissed me first
wanted to steal the sun
I just wanted to give you a quiet place
to heal
I am building a fort
made of amnesia
I am skilled in forgetting
I forgot you
hello
hello
the line is dead
the forest is burnt
letters can't plant trees
I went traveling
came back to a bouquet
of your flowers
a thousand trick questions
all the answers
wrong

we exploded
two sticks of dynamite
in a burning forest
you made the butcher's case
a case as old as Nigeria

I felt a close relative of shame
you left
I was never there
you brought the spring
from DC in your stomach
a change in the season
does not un-burn an entire forest
all the fires we experienced
but the ashes served as fertilizer
we promised to start
a small garden in Brooklyn
still thought we could steal the sun
I took out my daggers
worked on my amnesia
you read home and garden
I read playboy
a conflict was brewing.

Book III
SWAG OF SCARS
(2012-2013)

I can't breathe

I can't breathe
is not philosophical
or theoretical
it's a statement of fact
it's as American
as smallpox blankets
it's the underground railroad
catching its breath
it's the unit of measurement from
Dred Scott to Obama

I can't breathe
is not a literary device
though it is a metaphor
for all things black
for all things American
it's Sally Hemmings being
judiciously raped
by Thomas Jefferson
I can't breathe
is the first line of
the constitution
it's in the psychology
of every flag
stitched since Betsy Ross
in the fiber in every rope
braided by Klan hands
braided by the
United States
Supreme Court

I can't breathe
is the confederate flag
hung over a state house
in Alabama
in Mississippi

or on a Governor's lapel
I can't breathe
is the Dukes of Hazzard
the white citizen's council
it's separate but equal
it's every mask
every hood
every white sheet
every burning cross
every bombed church
every bullet riddled
black messiah
from here to Malcolm
from here to Garvey
from here to Nat Turner
from here to Crispus Attucks
it's 40 acres
of beautifully
manicured
poplar trees
bearing breathless
black corpses

I can't breathe
because 3/5 of the day
I am holding my breath
I suffer from a complex
called America
it's colorblind
therefore I am the
ghost in the machine
I am invisible
because it does not see race
yet it's racist as fuck
accused a 14 year black old boy
of stealing a state
so they could murder him

I can't breathe

is every moving image from
the birth of a nation
to the Zimmerman trial
it's the war on drugs
and I am the drug
it's the NRA and
it's standing its ground
it will stop you
and it will frisk you

dear black mothers
it is best if you started
giving birth
to oxygen tanks

I can't breathe
is not a mantra
not a prayer
it's an escape route
a cry for you to stop

I can't breathe
ain't nothing new
we been screaming it
since before the Mayflower
before the Amistad
before the Zong
it's etched
in every plank
that built Liberty Hall
in every block
that built the White House
the sound that split
the Liberty Bell

I can't breathe
is a black president
and a tea party
it's a black president

and a fox
who thinks
he is too smart
too uppity
for his own good

I can't breathe
is an American way of life
it's a wallet
a pack of cigarettes
a toy gun
a Walmart
a BART train
a cell phone
a stairwell
a fire lane
a car accident
a bachelor party
it's 6
it's 17
it's 41
it's 50
it's 138 fearful bullets
with no memory
of what took place
I can't breathe
because
America has me
in a chokehold.

Never give in

When all light
is slaughtered
when all memory
and love is
quarantined
when the day
no longer dreams
beautiful dreams
when the summation
of our fears outweigh
the thumping of
our courage
when there are
no words left
to say I love you
when all space
has receded
when all hope
has been expended
burnt and converted
to embers
even then, we still
won't surrender.

Basquiat

Braille teeth
dreaming in english
eating gunpowder
lipstick cello
robot orgasm
abstract hunters
to carve
artsy balance sheets
dying in french
reptile neon mistake
color blind drum
inner city mucus
metric whore
lamp
pill box
son of Van Gogh
eighty one
romance
invisible
super model midnight
silence
high.

Running with wolves

There are women
who sleep with swords
who set their beds on fire
and pray for rain
there a women
who would die before
I am sorry
a woman carpeted
in martyrdom
a dagger plunged
into her back
her own prints on it

then there are women
who are strong because
and beautiful for
and remembered always
who get praised
unsolicited
who run kingdoms
without effort
and they too sleep
with swords
and set beds on fire
but they do it
with honor
with grace
without spite

then there are women
who whore out their psyches
and sleep with gossip
and lie to themselves
then curse reality
and pray for heaven
when she created

hell.

Scars forget

Little girl, your heart
made of gold and dusty roads
memories of
a city
stellar
what happened
was it the screaming
correspondence from the
outskirts of tyranny
or the clay that conquered
the solitude lost
why the wretched songs
at morning?
why mourn for a still
breathing mother?

the rumbles
inside your eyes
a dictionary of
mis-defined terms

love isn't violent
it never bleeds roses
or rivers, or dinners
it heals wounds
I know there is no cure
for a wounded childhood
but I pray the salt water
helps.

Memories

Down memory lane we stroll
all the uncorrected ghosts
on park benches
coughing up secrets
regrets we can't
un-contrive
moments we can't undo
our hands bounded
by shame and
childhood deeds
evil deeds
we plan to pay for
with our children's ways

down memory lane we stroll
our umbrellas like
parachutes
to delicate the landing
to save us from
our mindlessly
unfinished dreams
to protect the soft
psyches we present
the manicured
feelings we have
packed away
in bubble wrap
like fine china.

Swag

Mouth of gold
you suck the devil's tailpipe
with such grace
it makes you Marlon Brando
James Dean-Hollywood cool
the sexy poison
escapes your nostrils
napalm erotic, yes
maybe this fire will get you
before the bullets do

laughing at the irony
the silly notion
of being murdered
by smoke, you suck it
with scorn, hatred even
observed it in silence
the grimace
the cold hugs your face
holds it tender
for a moment
you have become
the burning thing

this strange love
between your fingers
but you are Brad
cool as a fight club
with your latex life
surviving the ashes
ruined
at your feet
stranger still
both of you came
from the same field
metaphor?

no
just a slow lynch
infomercial for urban-death
I can see it now
a beautiful casket
with cigarette burns
included.

High noon

I hear the horses retreating
their hooves soldiering
in reverse
the bullets
re-casing themselves
mud jumping from
boot heel to earth

only songs now
and talk of peace
your heart was
always yours to break
my father
gave me
slippery hands
hence
I avoid guitars
light bulbs
and fragile women

crying fire
does not change
scripture
imagine you
with my hands
piloting a burning plane

the invisible
are the last to
know of invisibility
sad really
I saw the secrets
hiding under
your dress was
a den of vipers

a man bent on revenge
kills more of himself
than all the world's
armies on horseback.

Is it good

Blood brings
sharks with razor fins
misunderstood love
lions flesh fed to antelopes
dark oxidized blood
beautiful in the snow

diviners sanctuary
circles drawn
five paces
preparing for gunfire
explicit numerals
conflicting stories
crushed egos
it feels good
to tongue the scar?
let us pray it heals.

Monster

I am not monster
not fanged animal
soaked in primal force
fear and scruff
not brutal beast
not the dark thing
that murders
that crawls
and barks
and despises
not son of nightmare
with splinter
and shards for teeth

I am not memory lost
stories concocted
myth made stone
stone made holy
to smash skulls
not bitten tongue
sledge driving
nails through face
not claws or
arms ripped off
not severed eunuch
not mutilator
not mouth foul
with the smell of blood

not offspring of vampires
suffering from
delayed hate
not swallowed valium
blue knife conversing
with fucked bone
mangled in torture

swearing and spitting
up foam

I am not invisible
terror watching your
picket fence
not white body stuffed
into furnace
not ice pick
through ear drum
like smashed silk
no

I am steady
focused
smart
more human
than you
believe
but I'll be your monster
if it helps you heal.

Two questions

Have you ever seen
a bird singing
its final song
or a baby smiling
at nothing in particular

don't ever be that bird
don't ever forget how
to be that baby.

Bitten

She thought
this kiss
would last forever
overheard him being alive
bit into his tongue
held him there
the blood dancing
down, between
their bodies
still in a clasp

the why is most important
the flesh between
her teeth jumping
with life
the blood
the taste of his pain
her teeth
tightens until
the grinding sound
stalls her

the why is always important
but not now
she is busy
removing body parts
packing gun powder
in envelopes
writing letters to
whoever will confirm
her belief
that he too would leave
so she is building
a body
a brain
a heart

filled with pieces of the men
she has bitten into.

Last night

Skin radio
breath fingertips
notes shift
desire pressed
inward right
another chord
accordion darkness
digging skin
ear suggest
wine loosen
flesh novel
mysterious mouth

beautiful considered
chocolate apartment
coat palm
number squeezed
immoral reaching
tongues hearts
folded breast
possible release
autumn sprawled
melody swaying
swelling fingers
digging tongues
shoveling notes
heirloom removed
instrument licked
stockings torn
thought legs
extended sideways

raised eyebrow
pillow direction
moaning meaningful
heavy climbing

panting skin
sweaty lips
finger fruit
instrument hungry
pressed tasteful
yes
last
night.

Strange

Two men holding hands
in a church
love on their mind

two men holding guns
outside said church
murder on their mind

no rights for the former
more rights for the latter

strange.

Still

With tongue
she lit a lamp
at the end
of all darkness
her body covered
in hints of nothing
some innocent fantasy
maybe
ancient openings
giving birth to
themselves
vast continuums walking
through each other

ironic
how everything
was spoken
into being

contrary to
the standards
of dreams
there is no way
to prove
if we are awake
or asleep.

Never

No never is
because never is
never no
no is always no
zero
nothing
is never ever
not never mostly

a small star in a jar of butterflies
glow we be
the shedding of breath
the nth creation
unmaking still
the slow burn
embers
like galaxies french-kissing
a triplicate
dynamistic mention
toe even

a quasar itching
to walk across the brain space
slow, slow
eclectic sound fold
rigged up to the devil's math
simple
the lone metaphor
solo on third rib
fifth finger
music this
to invent so impossible a thing
it anti be
or ain't be it
but still is never.

Matador

There are rooms in her heart
places of subterranean love
emergency love
the whiskey ticket
a ceramic bowl of flaws
to charm this idiot
I am a fool for the things that destroy
the cleft of Dostoyevsky's pen
the grained curtain
she betrays her wings
a single horned visitor
on the balcony of autumn
something epic fermenting
through the generations

she has been many a walking instrument
some vague interpreter of shadows
the gun rack in the great room
praying for fallen men
they fall
the collectable they
wrong in manner and composition
they breath like an empty clown
drained of redemption
only to have her hand
to smile the way monsters do
unmoving still

they pray for a clearing in her heart
goddess of the parched form
she holds them
in broken places
through the expanse of
the machinery of her heart
she has studied
the face

knows its stereoscopic leanings
the physics of the thing that propels
she leads like a matador
constructed from fumes
into a world with a billion hearts
waiting to be broken.

Poets dream often

They dream of penning
metaphors
that will earn them the gallows
make them kings, saints, gods
they plot beneath
the bosoms of capita
garbed in pathetic scraps
Le Gran Marquis of poverty

the fingerless sons of liberty
dream of pens
dream of rebuilding Rome out of poems
writing from the thorax
from the quantum gut
philosophers of the drunken

born into the euphoria of
Keynesian economics
the Reagan years
with the beautiful odds
of being killed in the womb
by crack or crack mothers
victims of
the trickle down twitch

they dream of stardom
of stadiums filled
with screaming vaginas
limos of coke and
principled whores
the red carpet
the state funeral
the media hung up on their
breathing

they all dream of penning

brilliant poems
but they have no time to
go get the pen.

Killers

I have killed

yes, murdered
it is the murder
that makes us human

we have all done it
through some slight of ownership
some sub-primitive notion
of hoarding
or owning
another's being.

Nosedive

She will crawl
into his dreams
with her fantastic tattoos
her choked
ass like a sunrise over
a domed roof
professor of dangerous
flesh
hidden in the corridors of
sweet wordplay
academic nipples
limbs likes oiled snakes
sniper of stiff penetrating
circumstances
stalking her lover
on all fours
the sunrise
swallowing the thick
cleft of morning
she will find him
open him
with her juicy hands
and devour his flesh
suck the palpable
marrow from his bones
and easily
wipe all implied
abstractions
from her lips.

Big bang theory

We bang
we quote rope
we hope dark matter matters
fractals of factions
divided refrain
refraction
mixed reaction
theory of light
we move like fiction
two sickles, a cyclone
and a heroin addiction
one for the money
two for the motion
we build to break
bread fresh flesh
fermented in allure
or Allah covalent bonds
the molecular joined
multiplied
forced into
the outer
stellar cellular

we move like motion
we mobile
call it God, Allah or allure
opposites refract
light bends
call it prayer
even space prays
in the dim
for a flicker of understanding
the record rolls
it's all recorded
the needle skips
wait long enough

it comes back around
sound bends call it prayer
even belief believes
is it possible to not
be it as it weren't
we are all
daily
born anew
the record repeats
we have no choice
but to bang.

The letter twelve

He speaks through his teeth
like he got a mouth filled with
glass marbles
a mouth of excavated ovum
first drafts of the big bang
a simple truth
to wake god
to catch the sun exposed, like
his scavenged heart
thread bare lips
eyes drained of ears
imagination conquered

only circles here
mastered still
the ocean
bleeds
the night sky itself
under the cover of a subtle moon
they reflect equal distance
the songs different
the words changed
but the melody, constructed from
the same fiber
the same flesh
mortuaried by expired emotions

they give, like a
line down the middle of the street
two flags that won't surrender
so he speaks gently
through his teeth
hoping nothing brakes.

Signs

What do you do
when your country
does not want you

when the bread you are
made of
is not fit for the
tables of kings

until today
I never fully understood
the irony of
a WANTED sign
with the face of a man
who is a member of
the most UNWANTED
people on earth.

Hearts

Hearts are wet grinding trumpets
they ache, and dream
from mysterious angles
some small yellow bird
of a thousand meanings
singing in the chest

the heart astonishes sometimes
with its paper thin edges
hungry and screaming
troubled harmonies
like a village on fire
or a heat wave of eagles
important though
is the heart's calling
its brutal knocking
the rumors it pounds out

it sniffs through
the crackling agonies
of a universe that meanders
like the spirit of children
the way it unquenches
the bleeding madness
of attempted assassinations
the heart wears
mirrors
beautiful mirrors
it thrashes
until it is rock
or unfinished Jell-O

the heart circles
in the sky
waiting for revenge
and murders, noisy murders

154

with its lantern eyes
and nightmare grin
but also
the heart loves.

Kids *(for Tupac & BIG)*

They were kids
making music
out of the crack epidemic
post-modern
couriers of sabotage
of hate crafted steel
and mounds of coke
shaped like klansmen
smelling like
the ricochet
of Malcolm's last breath
off the shell casings
like Banneker's letter
to Thomas Jefferson
written in the darkest dye

you carved up the charts
sold synthetic murder to
white America
like penny stocks
fed black bodies
to funeral homes
like penny stocks
no Lincoln to save us
no Gettysburg address
when Baltimore is Gaza
when Bed-Stuy is Rhodesia
and murder camp
no truth to deny the beat

a people, assassinated by
a menagerie of lies
we all danced
swallowed spirits
rolled up blunts
nodded as if confirming

yes
yo momma was a Panther
yo momma knew Garvey
and you don't stop
the Catholic church must be proud
all those dance lessons locked
behind bars
the irony is
Jesus died at 33
you outdid Christ
looked better on the cross
like you were posing for pictures
they said you never died
immortality in a hail of bullets
you would have named them
after your songs
Dear Momma
Keep Ya Head Up
I'm Ready To Die
sadly, there is nothing noble
about dying at 25
you sold more than the Bible
god, you could have been Messiah
but the epidemic was too sexy
couldn't see past the tight dress
so you bit into the apple
the snake got you.

Yow son

Yankee hat
Jordans
durag
skinny trues
fresh braids
black hoody
pants below ass
neck tattoo
forearm tattoo
exposed boxer.
"is that your son"
"nah, that's my daughter"
"how old is she"
"eleven months"
"how old are you"
"16"
a long pause
"when she is 16 I'll be 32"
"wow."

Book IV

SORCERER'S DAUGHTER

(2011-2012)

Charmer

Bewitcher
sorceress
deviled soft skinned
snake hips
cruel, cruel eyes
lips of Lucifer
you walk like
engineered spite
you wicked woman you
why must you own
the earth with every roll
of your ass
every stumble of
midnight flesh
Rembrandt must have
inked you woman
seducer of a previous mortality
we have crossed paths before
damn you
why did you dig up my bones
to have me recognize you
I am a dog at your feet
and if ever the conditions were right
I would love to aquarium you
to eloquently orate a small
section of your sky
remove this gash of heart
this imagined love is
destroying me
like a
dawning cholera.

Father

The wind whistles
through his open wounds
he calls them poems
he is trying to drink the pistol
away from his head
his life, a series of head on
collisions he
dreams in seat belts
made out of pieces of his
fragmented father

awake, he is matador
asleep he is stadia
the world loves a wounded animal
bull's blood mostly
maybe it's the life released
or the beauty of the blood
sliding recklessly
down the hopeless face
of the thing expired

dear father it is so hard
to out believe a train
or a wall
they tend not to move
won't make way
they think themselves
permanent
there is no surgery for gone fathers
or rejection
like you father
I am a father now.

Luminae

They found him
in a pitch black room
pouring books into his brain
ingesting liquefied scrolls
memorizing versions of god
his sweat in a pool below
formed drawings
from a different age
a different time he
bled a soft light
a map
of the human psyche
around his dome
a heart shaped halo
of dreams.

Free

We, commune like tsars
fly like sars
bird flu
word flew
word you was king kong
still strong
they try to herb you
sage, so they burn you
on crosses, god body
third level
third devil
grape vine
bloodline
coming from a
great lion
sheep
they try to herd you
placebo plebian
pushed to the corner
lock down forever for
a pound of marijuana

illegal regal
king with the bling
now
story stay deep
we lord of the rings now
selfish shell fish
lobsters mobsters
gang sign wrong sign
vision filled with trouble
could have been the Hubble
space man space ship
crawling to the slave ship
same shit nah son
could have been a mystic

rather be a monster
invisible, invisible
myth of the 3/5
working on our fractions
fractured on the block
like a chemical reaction
auction on lock
we perm
and burn herbs
use verbs to calm nerves
we turn words into fiction
blurs into diction
dread on the corner
selling the heroin addiction
selling stock futures
used to be livestock
now he sells the live rock
fractured his mind
yep, fractured he's blind.

Little girl with a dead moth

She held it
in her frown
her cupped hands
and eyes quizzed by
this unspeakable act
a garden of worries
in her brow
a furrowed question
then an utterance
"why isn't it moving?"

Tightrope I

This body
whiskey ballerinas its way
through poems
like some failed truth
a stumbling paper factory
of reckless books
of scribbled relatives
relatives are minefields
of gathered asylums
father saunters through her dreams
he speaks the taste of her lips
thighs, confetti tongue, lungs
throat stitched
askew
raw
you smell the scars
charred and lumpy.

Tightrope II

This body
a tortured cinema
a thousand beds
filled with ashtrays
children with blue grey
smoke for hair
nothing to quench
the things we believe
or intend
searching for
the torn scattered
pieces of Antigone
nothing to undream the
monstrous undertaking
no vodka strong enough
to murder the self
or the gods we doubt
mouths all Dante
all razor
and insecure
wombs set to repeat
to solar flare
to speed dial the kill switch
to wipe out all semblance
of the future
abort the saint
wrist in a full sprint
dreaming at Mach 3
dying at Mach 10
like an earthquake
with a ruptured lung
a baptist church in a cod piece
with god in the pews
engulfed in memoir
rapt in so many invisible things.

Tightrope IV

Maybe this poem
could save her
could save him
stop the bleeding
this blood is relative
bleeding relatives
with
subtext
pretext
plots
heroes
villains
we are all monsters
hypocrites of the kill song
rogue actors
doctored scripts
we dance gracefully
on the killing floor
Roberta need not sing
of the shredded child stuffed
in her mouth
the flesh
swallowed of all meaning
is ugly
all she ever wanted to be
was ugly
and loved
all he ever wanted to do, was
to feel human in the smoke
to scream like a rabid ape
to be alive and pure
to express
to meet a billion incarnations
of something simple.

Chess players

They gather
these dark figures
on park benches
to grapple with possibilities
to square the truth
chain-smoke fingers
sacraments of the green earth
move like nightfall
it smells like Ashanti kingdom
eyes, relics from the
empire of gold
they cough a lung here
a ship there
some antiquated decree
their memories like
thin slivers of calcified stone
they indulge
move in and out of
consciousness
the language
beautiful with its sharp edges
masters at mastering
the art of wooden statues
they sit, think, move
this, not mere ritual
they study
the craft
of shit talk
every word
a cathedral to the highest of art
to the science of entering
a man's mind
and telling him what to do next
"white piece moves first."

Believers

When babies
speak of divinity
when the land protests
our being here
where there is no place
for the homeless
to be homeless
when the night is lit
perpetual neon
when our dreams
are produced by
machines
then and only then
we will know
we have gone too far.

Below ground

Everything echoes
drawings
stick figures
smiles erased
amalgamated
Africans
humanoid
ancient
architects
their hands
their overexposed
lifemares
cast them as wooden
sculptures
sanctified stones
that breathe
beauty into chaos
a study of incredible
markings
a noble river
sliding to the house
of non-believers
a modern weapon
overflowing with
stillness like
a conquered painting
a captured minute
a chalice of odes
their eyes
unique
lips
the source
disciples of the metal vein
they move
underground

for fear of competing
with the sun.

Overdose

I want to be the
first person who overdoses
on not believing.

Chalk

A smile
a child with a gun
for mouth
a sky painted human
the sun dances
moves
to open us
to verse us
like Bibles be
the door that
unlocks breath
the sound that un-nails dreams
we dream sky
tell stars of elephants
our scribbled voices
on canvas
even in sickness
never silent
our pens race
they feel and tell
inspire and open
shrink and expand
through time
we tumble
we now.

Fire

The tease was easy
maybe it was the softness
a giggling satisfaction
this lone orchid
inside a stampede of
poison ivy
they snake about her
she walks like
autumn
no Bible
no Koran
no ancient text
can explain how she felt
me looking
knew I suffered from some
innocent desire to know her name
to draw stories across
her narrative of limbs
no parable could explain
how she knew me
before we met
my heart grabbing for wires
I was lamplight
she is six feet of goddess
I am cast-iron
in sea water
I kissed myself good bye
meet you at the bottom
amongst the stones.

Ink

Beautiful
she moves subtle
her contemplated skin
is a dark jar of gazelles
frozen in midair
a statue sculpted
from things we can
only remember
tasting
right there
the fumbled traces
roots all coconut musk
and ancient chants
limbs, hips, body and breast
alight in this orange glow
she is altar
and gate, and grave
a holy thing
flesh like scripture
for my palms to read
some future fruit
fallen from an imagined
heaven, ripened
she promised to lick the
prints from my fingers
to name every bone in her body
after each breath we took
in the undertaking
composed a song of tongues
and heavy breathing
we called it hallelujah.

The devil

The devil is a dream
invented by
men with tongues that
de-vein the psyche
you, flushed with fear
no heaven underneath
god is a chain reaction
that moves from
book to book

it's in our blood
the darkness bred it
back then
when all
that existed was
brutality and murder
so now we crave heaven
like addiction

breathing is prayer enough
don't forget, god is only
6000 years old
hiding in some far corner...
defying physics
un-balling logic
I imagine he is thoroughly
concerned with your lady parts
has "to do booklets"
on how to package ones
virginity
how to be against god
and all things natural

go find your breathing
and share it with someone
or something beautiful.

The city

The city hulks
toward the gift of stars
heads swirling
the revelers screaming
all the obscenities
we know
murder lodged in the maw
we trumpet meaninglessness
babble
songs to end
all things true
the night is a lie
diseased memory
cratered love
toppled scars
sheet music for beggars
their arms a lexicon
of statutory survival
4 am
we march toward our graves
neon zombies, of light
and slurred speech
platform sign
next train to Brooklyn
31 minutes.

Plastique

At first the surgery
turned my stomach
the knife abandoned on your face
body pumped with silicon
your breasts pretending
they knew my mouth
this betrayed
science of happiness
Los Angeles
your texture
annoys and charms
pages slowly through me
I am falling in love
hate you for it
angels aren't supposed
to whore themselves
should never be
this high
this early.

Freescience

Unlocking candles
light for the masses
unlocking angles
today's mathematics
star spangled night sky
flow like it's wi-fi
sick with the abstract
move folk like Amtrak
born black
die black
can't leave this shit bitch
you guaranteed to relapse
relax
chill and
somebody go' notice
focus
focus
green like it's locust
love for the love of love
desida...what the fuck
fuckas love to pray
I'm sitting here like... what tha fuck
can't fuck with yo god above
and keep your white jesus
fuck it I'm the god within
speaking to the god within
all you need is confidence
fuck em and they consequence
so I keep it on the abstract
move folk like Amtrak
born black
die black
that should be your way back.

Orchid

Dear orchid
we were once in full bloom
a sun at midnight
we pulled the water
back and forth like tide
days in that valley
nightmares exposed
a perfectly painted boy
on a crowded gravel road
it's just him held hostage
by the painters imagination
I am sorry, the earth turned its back
on you
dry soil and saliva
have always been enemies
I am afraid of friends
you were easy to walk away from
especially with a mouth
full of molten razor blades
only if our hearts were
less brimstone and more
like the love of a newborn's
smile
it makes no sense blaming
the morning for the fog
or the change of weather
constants are never constant
forgive the grass
for we are all grass
our blades sometime
murder others by accident
cause is often mistaken
for intent
content mistaken for malice
I love every dream in your body
every evening

that falls from your lips
orchid
what happened to our planned dreams
we said forever
signed it in a cradle of blossoms
then we drew our swords
I have no heart left
only a place where the ashes
grits its teeth and snarls
at the ticking clock
can a day be undone
no
I have seen men
surrounded by a confederacy
who could never understand
flight or wings
only funeral pyres
and darkest hades
we
you and I
sired a poem
that rhymed with everything
now nothing?
not even heaven can un-draw
this line
this black line down the center of you
remember?
we can't lie to the universe
the universe has no middle
only a place for fingers to point
for whispers to stir
for monsters to pretend
they come with artificial names
and temporary cunning
I say we walk away from the chatter
the tide will wash
the lines from the sand.

Inglewood

Inglewood
is bottom bitch
will suck and fuck the poor
for free
'round the back parts of
Marylin's Soulfood, on Crenshaw
her weave
a plantation of churches on fire
check out the pock marks
her pogrom heart
set to permanent hoe stroll
she will sell her last child for a fix
who will fix her
give her light
no, give her candle
slide that economic needle
into her vein
hope she can nod off this reaganomics
ain't shit trickling down from
Baldwin Hills
no beautiful poems about
Harlem or novels contrived
in Paris
check out
Inglewood
fucking up the view
Inglewood
a nuanced retrospective
of Alabama 1784
the row houses
smelling like tobacco fields
like blocks of solid white
cotton the street lights dim
a moon hung low
black faces decorated
with sorrow

but they smile
as if their middle name
was renaissance
it can't get no worse
the mayor is spitting
watermelon seeds like
friendly fire
for the curators of the
affordable casket museum
Inglewood
I pray the needle brakes
the lamp tips
and burns this bitch down
that the smoke chokes your pimp
and fucks him slowly
down his dick.

Song

Songs happen upon
their creators
some songs are hits
others are loud or annoying
quiet songs are the best
will move you to tears
especially when she smiles.

Friend

To find a friend
with a heart this kind
this honest
the distance distorts
the continent warped
dali-esque
face painted
abacus
cartouche bracelet
naming ceremony
eyes like a bolt of beautiful
sitting inside a cup
of warm smoke
on the sidewalk for tea
herbal
dinner slides by still
the keys repeating
as the poem sprints
like a promise through the brain
I know
honest hearts are rare
the fury of love often
destroys the best of them
the conundrum of living
complicates pure
so I say
thank you
universe.

Trapped

Your music is beautiful
your instrument a collection of
emotions, an orchestra
playing steady-like
but to parachute
to sure death
onto the perfected
blade of an axe
this act of self-murder and
self-resurrection
evident in these instruments
strip mining tears
the trembling lips
the gut feeling crawling
through the blood
a stick of dynamite
between the teeth
beneath the tongue
you are a rogue messiah
straying out of the pages of
a holy book
to teach these
brass flutes
how to walk on water
to turn pain into wine
to pull bread from stone
to feed the masses
this is an act of god
the sacrificed lamb
risen
yes
this is no metaphor.

Book V
SPELLCASTER'S MANUAL
(2010-2011)

The Heart

Hearts are wet
grinding trumpets
the ache we dream
from mysterious angles
some small yellow bird
of a thousand meanings
singing in the chest
the heart astonishes sometimes
with its paper thin edges
screaming troubled
harmonies
like a village on fire
like boiling water
or a heat wave of eagles
important though
is the heart's calling
the rumors it pounds out
it sniffs through the crackling
agonies of a universe that meanders
the way it unclenches
the bleeding madness
of attempted assassinations
the heart wears
mirrors
beautiful mirrors
it thrashes until it is rock
or unfinished jell-o
the heart circles in the sky
waiting for revenge
murder noisy murder
with its lantern eyes
nightmare grin
but also the heart loves.

Sorceress

Funny you said you are
a normal person
sorceress
all that coy
isn't natural
like you have lived this moment
a few times
your smile, holding back
an eon of circling hurricanes
fingers dancing the flesh
what is it you are not saying
I feel the microbes moving
in you
your lips
a misquoted scripture
something like a suicide note
we could move Monday
and father a village
of star children
who will speak in blurred
paintings
we could blur the night
turn heaven into a
beautiful ritual of sheets
deify each other
we can be god together
turn that water into wine
me Trismegistus
you Hera
a different age
a different time
you a bird of paradise
I, flash photography
just beholding you
may be enough

but when has enough
ever been enough.

Great Britain

What did you expect
of this breed of
Nintendo children
the ones borne
out of cannons
their monstrous hearts
carrying the contents
of the Enola Gay
their eyes bearing the insignia
of McDonalds
they who will climax in your murder
the same as you, in lands afar
their delicious cocktails
to light the skies
they did it for the fame
to feel relevant
to feel as if they too exist
they did it screaming
fuck William and Kate
I too have meaning
"look ma I'm on TV..."
these misguided sons of the crown
to them these fires are imagined
they will press reset
in the morning
and return to their
gorgeous baaing.

Dear Troy *(for Troy Davis)*

Dear Troy
it's Georgia
it's the south
it's America
something about
state's rights
something about
almost human
you were real estate
cargo
from the stone fleet
the wildfire
Madre de Deus
La Amistad
ships filled with
fine-tuned slaughter
lethally injected into
Georgia, America
all the valium in the world
won't calm their nerves
Georgia knows
how deep
does one have to dig
to bury a slave ship?
but the stench, oh the stench
is a beautiful monument

dear Troy
I envy you
congratulations
on your visibility
I know nothing of the weapon
or the alchemy of court rooms
the calculus of legal phrasing
but something feels wrong
in the congress of my stomach

some unexploded frenzy of darkness
I wondered if my words
would have been as poetic
knowing I was being culled
as a back room audition
at some sick carnival
the irony of an uneven death
on the most balanced
day on the calendar
I imagined the judge's fingers
soaked in tobacco stains
his brow furrowed
rolling his tongue around the tip
of a long black cigar
the smell of fruit ripened by summer
walks gently through his dreamy head
as he signs your death warrant

Georgia On My Mind
being sung by Ray Charles
in the back
ground
and in that rudimentary motion
something catches
inside his chest
as he realizes he is signing his own
death warrant
and the blood riffling through
the brandy in his veins stops
he catches a tear
before it hits the page
in this lonely act of denial
it hits him
I AM A MONSTER.

Linguist

Your language
the metaphor
words
your tongue
so gentle
this craft
moves realms
metaphysics?
holy?
this language
metaphor
word
word
your tongue
so gentle
this craft
is it possible to paint
a heartbeat with the tongue
to melt belief with language
to raise the dead with sound
to transmute a stick of dynamite
into a sigh of relief
this language
metaphor
word is word
your tongue
a camera
a light projector
a factory for spoken
does the tongue dream?
this craft
a ship of a thousand tongues
did we really speak the stars into the sky?
or the crude construction of who we are
spoken clay
languaged into being

a linguist
maybe
a metaphor
a word
yes.

The not dreamer

It is easy to not dream
to stifle the million breaths
you take
oh sweet killer
brandy glazed eyes
trouble sharpened teeth
that you are
hands callused
by weed smoke
and spliff tails
a cycle of perpetual suicide failures
you jump at every siren
every skirt
you got the art of bullshit
all science lab methodic
all that swag lost in a cloud
mis-remembered street hustlers
of terrifying smoke
I guess
this is the preamble
to the day the bullets
come wheezing
their awkward selves
into the collected myths of
who you claim to be
to tear you heaven and such
bleed you unnecessary
make you a logo
for the boys to
pour to
this corner
negotiated sacred space
to chalk your self-portrait
erect an altar
a tombstone
for your baby sister to kiss

the spliff quivers
under your fumbled speech
your eyes say
fuck your dreams.

Check one

To be this black on purpose
is to be a king cut in half
a shaman grounded by
a contortion of snakes

the gun-less are baffled by
the murderous carriers of heaven
let me clean that gun for you sah
spit shine its echo

all those ships
on the front page of
the New York Times
in beautiful fine print
times roman
a fiery multiplication of empires
I'll just draw the coffins now
mayday, mayday
labor for free
labor
the smuggled truth
in a midnight factory
of a billion shangos
mayday, mayday
I am in possession of a smile
I perform
the inferior task
of being
remember they love you
with a horn in your mouth
or pig skin for a funeral
Miles pressed atop Cicely
barely breathing
blame Hannibal at the gates of Rome
Charlie Parker choking on his horn
a refurbished battle cry

coughing up the 9th ward
Jack was king, swinging
fucked more white girls
than he got credit for
fucked up more white boys
than we care to remember
so we pray to the exploded
carcass of William S
some surrealist ape in a suit
with a gun in his mouth
all that language
and not a word
of the terror
a long line of blind men
partaking in the most
democratic of rapes.

Twice

A roused circle
a wooden bridge across
a dark canyon
a caressed sky
a canvas of moans
ritual bliss
buckets full
her inner inquiry
caught by impulse
a manuscript of hip rotation
slow down baby
that's before we got all
evangelical and she was
reverend promises
and yes right there
and I was
the ridiculous mister eleven
leg cramps and repentance
sweat and testimony
kissed Bible and
midnight prayers
but, when the sunlight
hit the back of the river
we were two notes
dangerous and graceful
her sighs like poetry
we wrote until
our resonance
had no reason
instruments crying
for all the known gods
of flesh and struggle
of love and nightmares
of galloping
extraordinary sensations
something to split you

beautiful
to painfully open
the brutal parts
of us both
to leave us glassy eyed
and heavy limbed.

Capital-ism

An easy dinner with
a murder of crows
a premeditated coffin on fire
they sip the flesh
from the bone
statutory robbery
inhumane arson
of spirit
the mass markets slaughter
the charred remains
of those most deserving
of those spoiled or marred
by the tenor of simpletons.

Lady in red

Eyes like
well-trained violins
just the right note
keys gently pushed
a hovering
ceremony of silk red lips
pressed against this
rogue heart
this feels more like
perhaps

some old dominion
from a century of traditions
whispered into
the matrimony
of hands
Virgina with all its brilliant soil
could not house you or
the fury of your smile
you eventually came with
a head of dreams spilling across
the Mason Dixon
with one thought burning
in your brain
where did you get that skin?

Yes

One hand
to walk the flesh
to catch the sprouted stem
to incredible the boulevard
pirate the continent
of hooded offerings
ribbons of pressed peaches
the fingers question
the abstained bouquet of
deepest devil
the spread spectrum
riverbed garden smooth
as ceramic in dew
a pocket full of petals
to critique until the lips quiver
arrow shot through a
passing memory
the smell of clouds
and quicksilver
of muscle and gently
bruised fruit.

Until tomorrow

The night moves
into the glass of my chest
like a bottle of wine
the best of both worlds
swirled slowly
swallowed
like Jonah
deep inside the belly
of a whale
to be spat out
like sacred prayers
two days later
and still no god in the sky
to remove the handsome smell
of her from his fingers
or from this glass
at his lips
the night is dizzy with desire
brimming to explode
like a stick of something
needed
a slow song to keep the tempo
a small oven to fan the flames
as it meanders up the spine
every disc a cypher
covered in want
a succulent stroke from the clock
wakes the dead
the cock crows
as we moved out into the night air
the smell of morning
pressed against our flesh.

Broken Basquiat

These paintings
are your dreams
vacuumed out of you
the murder-saw hacking
through, drained you beautifully
black god that you are
you fought, yes
but the parable is scavenger
it will eat you
to be merchandise and king is rare
still you smiled
painted the laundered silence
of the blood empire
their knell, homeless
their knives over your head
these creatures of habitual
slaughter
your brush
a museum of ancestors
dimensional, self-mutilation
a noose in every stroke
a drum turned field song
turn gospel, turn Charlie Parker
or a hoard of bucking horses
still you smiled
you took tea
knowing they were sharpening
the Guggenheim
champagne with your ashes
primate
prime-time
primary-colors
primal
what a word
when they opened you
on the steel table

I wonder what was
the cause of death
I heard you overdosed
on racism...
on a blackness
more wretched than
your father's love.

High science

Somehow the birds
knew the storm
was coming
the trees were empty
of their noises
they all got the message
without a single tweet.

My generation

The men of my generation
who bleed truth
are snatched at the dirtiest
parts of night
their ripe corpses
clothed in a stony sweat
in the back of shiny white limos
its morgue-like eyes
heavy with segregation
they go unnoticed
a catastrophe of nuns
could not pray them visible
their faces like brutal blades
fiery eyes to burn halos
through all things sacred
they scrape and dig
into these facades
in search of something humane
to hug
to hold on to
to feel human with
they enter the mass transit
a reckless assault of glitches
heavy with rewiring
the pain sucked
for salt

lean limbs
to nullify the rope
or cancel out gravity
the humming
that cancer
the self
that needs the light
tha

t small flicker of dream
the hammer, a personal friend
grotesque against that dark skin
they move
all pretense
and calloused palms
sable vampire hearts
the men of my generation
are lazy drooling monsters
clamoring at your wives
begging for the mercy
of their beds
or their cold witch snatches
oh to slide two uncircumcised fingers
into her careless purse
I have seen the men of my generation
strung out on reaganomics
when brownstones morphed into graves
the boys they birthed
are regaled in beautiful gang colors
their hand signs
medals of valor
their gold fronts
the armor of gladiators
titans even
they embrace death
and prisons like fathers
loose women, alcohol and thick
medicated smoke
to cancer them away
if even for a tick
a ritual
a rite of passage
a path toward some
blurry phantom
manhood
or a possible
escape from these
stinking fuckin' projects

they claim like ceded lands
building 3
yeah
that's home
with all its mechanical failings.

Asylum

To love is asylum
absinthe mixed with venom
yet we leap
against probability
we fall into and through
each other
if only to seal the hole
torn by our last attack
that morning
you woke up limping
your heart had been secreted
out of your chest
by a sexy faced thief
the gash marks
a surgical crucifixion
there she goes
with two hearts beating
beneath her polished smile
the cure
is loneliness
eat your heartbreaks
and learn how to murder
those closest
to your heart.

Protesters *(Occupy Wall Street)*

Dear protesters
it is best to dream
after you die
the democracy of dreams
is impractical
especially in the belly
of a machine trying to prove
it can eat its children
eventually they will
have you sautéed
with asparagus
you screaming
your moral code does not stop
their knives, congratulating
your spine and all the soft places
you own
this poem is meant to de-moral-ize you
to wake you up
stop dreaming
ask the man of inked skin
still in the throes of an
unfractioning
mentored by
the republic's blade
he has achieved a singular
invisibility
from four centuries of dreaming
ask the "natives"
what happened
when they met the dexterity
of capitalism
from sea to shining sea, baby
now it's your turn
they will free market
laissez-faire fuck you to chalk
with a civilized slice of media

a dollop of republican dogma
so it goes down easy
the luxury of
un-horning a raging bull
is always placed in the hands of the young

they...
they will be our monks on fire
our olympians with raised fists
our conscientious objectors
judiciously starving themselves
their dangerous bones
stuck into the eyes
of king and crown
of Proctor and Gamble
of Goldman and Sachs
they will come
as if they inherited
some magnificent hallelujah
instruments raised high
trumpets and drums
maracas and bells

with the pyrotechnics of tongues
clown suits and hula hoops
prayers and poems about possibilities
giant vision and futures
themes and beautiful songs
their voices
a raspy cathedral of resist
a contingency of actualizers
men of science and waged laborers
dish washers and doctors
unionists and entrepreneurs
designers and nurses
teachers and clerks
lawyers and artists
with crude demands for equality
with shameless brutal demands for equality

with barbaric evil demands for equality

these...these are our children
they fight our wars
murder on our behalf
they dreamt up the mechanics of
this new commerce
you used to slaughter them
yet their sleep is for sale
their bread and health hedged
against a sacred tax loophole
dear Wall Street
you need new clothes.

Her heart

Her heart is a gentle thing
a block of solid rock
nothing gets in
nothing gets out
but here she is
professed
in the art
of loving him still.

Song

He thinks her
a song
she thinks him
a sunny morning
they are planning to make
eternity
he thinks she
is normal
she thinks
he is canine
they face the wall

he thinks her
a monster
she thinks
he a thunderstorm
they are both submerged
in blue
he thinks her
potential peace
she thinks
he is married
they left her music
in his bed
he thinks her
history

she said
he is father
but the
DNA belongs to another.

Painting

A brush filled with languages
with body songs
with cryptic chemistry
grounded marble
metal shavings and blood
the masters drifting in and out of
moonlit prisms
this strange literature
of colors
flicked wrist
stumbled calligraphy
of random
hands carried by ghosts
a golden key to open
heart and bone
peer up through the floorboards
of belief
maybe I'll find god
lost along a
pathway through my head
slice by slice the
world comes back into focus
the brush moves
argues softly with the canvas.

The art of handling snakes

It is impossible
for a snake to swallow
its own head
the exploits of snakes
are limited
to self-survival

snakes are not immune
to venom
their composed parts
are gentle

the irony of being
encased in a dangerous
fragile body
is a tragic metaphor.

Itch

All day
I dream of her
of having her thin frame
pressed against a wall
or on the floor
working every inch
of her surface
in tones and colors
of heightened roughness
to achieve a visible dripping and pouring
to watch her body
catch the light
canvas her every texture
sanctified holy
the rhythm of thick full strokes
of intense intangible
under currents
this is about technique
about opening
spaces and disappearing
deep inside
the overlapping.

Banker's toast

Let's
toast to the poor saps
who we duped
the silly nations
that think us friend
oh the beautiful rapes
we have committed
this buffet of unemployed are
meals prepared
we'll spoon them into perpetual
poverty soon
the smell of economic collapse
has my trouser stiff with starch
and things I can't mention
oh my brothers in arms
have you seen
the silly kids
in the streets
they speak of justice
that succulent whore
of ours
I wonder if they know
we invented her
can they see around corners
the way we do
I hope they are dreaming
of the canopy of batons
we have in store
the riot police
the tear gas
the men on horseback
I hope they have had visions
of the preach of blood
and bullets that will silence
their songs

to the saps brothers
to the saps.

All she wanted

All her lonely hips needed
was a song
a guttural song
a song to destroy all she
knew of him
to stretch her past
all human things
a song of glittering terror
a cold emotionless song
a savage song
of cerebral kidnapping
with a meaningless ending
a song she could call messiah
if only for a moment
a strange song to unhook
the anchor he left
to tear the roots out
and shake off all that
soil
I could not sing
so, I wrote her a luscious poem
we journeyed past the convulsions
woke up on the other side
of summer
with our bodies swearing.

Circus *(for Occupy Wall Street)*

Embers fly
from Brooklyn Bridge to
Golden Gate
a heart in flames
a saber tooth babble
shiny towers
encased in suspicion
the shouts
eyes filled with fiery
disobedience
the bodies worked
into a crescendo
a mob of copycats
they wear the same pain
the truth on vacation
the lie televised
mass marketed
to the lowest fool
liberty is sleeping pill
a love affair with poverty
a circus with no pitched tents
mic check
the mayor of bull horn
with his cadre of idiots
they traffic silence
arm themselves with
scars
so go ahead
form a line and get your head split.

Africa at work

She dragged it all in
like the Congo
all that Zambezi
all crouched
in her lap like a black
catastrophe
got me thinking
I need to go home.

Preppy pimp (Halloween)

Look at him
practicing his back-hand
his slick grimace
imagining he can bitch slap
tha bijesus outta some silly
fuckin trick
his swag
reflected in the vast
glass pane of Trump Soho
pop that collar playa
drag that fucking leg
walk like that dick heavy
hat to the side
bell bottoms like a
retro-active murder
corduroy and denim combo
check ya tone bitch
watch her flinch
at your breathing
yeah that's it playa
you a true pimp
but I have a question
do you know what it is that
pimps do?
maybe you do
why else would you wear
a pimp's uniform
to a party of monsters.

Dear Herman (for Herman Cain)

Carrying wood
jolly to the pyre
braiding rope
for the inevitable lynch
stirring tar
for the holy scorch
feathers to angel the burns
we have come full circle
you are
a confederate flag
made out of cowrie shells
Herman
Igbo
Herman
Fulani
Herman
Ashanti
Herman
Fanti
it took a whole lot
of selling to get us here
many a forked
tongue
the lies piled high
vampire state
999 what a metaphor
you are Elegba
without knowing
without knowing
Shango with no teeth
no sword
just a slice of pizza
a pedophilic smile
and a sales pitch.

230

Light

The light falls
in thin slits
through the clouds
visits your bed
transmutes your body
into a shrine
a holy place
the ripples
the contours
and dips
a landscape of skin
perfect now
perfect ever
angel in bloom
in your bed of
light
I worship nights
but I pray for morning.

White girl with a fat ass

You flaunt it
like you invented
breathing
they say it's
Africa at work
say the water got
that dark DNA in it
brothers love you
for your fat ass
for the wonder
for the exaggerated muscle
the tension squeezed
into a Mm.
a damn
the holy sepulcher
plagued by questions
no one ever asks
where you were educated
you never say
it is easier to live
within the curvature
of a small box
than to expose yourself
to the grail of being
fully human
yeah
you got a fat ass
but what do you think
about poverty in America
spiritual poverty.

Glass heart

You fed her
fruit infused
poetry
watched her novel
herself into
a mumbled oath
forever?
no
she wants to be
more than memory
you wanted her light
your pencil broke
in the pungent
smell
of her
notebook
now what?

BIG as always

Dear Voletta
for you
Brooklyn is either
graveyard or museum
the impact of your son
bruises all walls
they temple him here
god him out of stone
his image trapped
behind the impact
of steel and dreams
when the paint fades
and we forget
you will hold him
a mental picture
in the gentrified sprawl
the county of KINGS
land of a million poets
street soldiers salute the tragedy
of the language he possessed
all that possibility
clouded in swag
maybe per chance Voletta
had we met in a cypher
a poem could have saved him
we poets are that optimistic
or, that egotistical
we build and save
maybe not a poem
a sermon of prose perhaps
for he was a poem
and it is rare for one poem
to save another
even now
I can see him
bobbing in the dracula

of the booth
the entire literature
of his being
saying
"It was all a dream."

Screw face

Your grimace
seems prescribed
an exaggerated dagger plunge into
the loneliness of night
you vs the fury of love
I can hear your teeth grinding
this bent face
like a weapon
pressed against
your temple
this ruthless art
maybe there is a heaven
in there somewhere
I wish you wings.

Move on

When the darkness
is manufactured
the truth stretched
the scars tailored
and mass marketed
there is a given ire
a pretend zeal
about a morgue filled
with lovers
who victimed you
the exposed bone
documents the pain
the cadence of
a clutched heart
is music struck down
by a brutal hammer
but pain is a form of art
music is a form of pain
so the love you owned
or lost
constructs us
beautifully
shapes us easy
but, gratitude is light.

Sight

We wrestled
palms full of sheet
gripped the momentum
did everything
but breathe
held our breaths
and listened
to the dark
circle our tumbling
until the spasms
came a walking
down our spines
the satisfaction
left me a blind man.

Vision

A blind man
sees what is necessary
to survive.

Homeless

The stench is
Rembrandt-esque
he is a soft charcoal
a chemical reaction, frozen
a tattered religion
a piece of classical music
composed from straw
a crippled infinity
turned in on itself
a quantum paradox
reaching out into a field
of splintered eyes
his existence violent
against the morning commute
the smell regal in
its full bodied putridity
he is high fashion
in this sea of
biological waste
his eyes and gait
rains hatred
look at them, he thinks
robots all
he, a fully realized
civilization
a post-modern shaman
a human galaxy
viewed as homeless
how can one be homeless
when the universe is all
around us?

Herman caned

Herman
how does it feel
having your teeth checked
your balls and genitals
resting gentle
betwixt the vice-grip's teeth
there is something
agrarian in the way
they undress you
you have not caught on
you, in the monster's uniform
wearing the monster's history
all that black and them pearly whites
have always been reserved for
the kitchen not the bedroom
for the slave quarters not hotels
for 12 years she walked around
with Emmet Till's eyes in her purse
I wonder how long before
the addiction kicked in
you, so far drawn from Malcolm
you, could have been Garvey's dad
you, caught with your snout
sniffing around in
that sweet barrel of
gun powder
your skin is flint
be careful you don't get swine flu
Herman, you
go too easily
into the animal's mouth
chant their beliefs
like scripture in Mecca
they were all blonde
weren't they?
welcome to the BBQ

you volunteered
to be lynched
to be chopped finely and stuffed
into a tight space
you say it's hard being
black and conservative
imagine how hard it is
being black and thoughtful.

Singer (for Imani Uzuri)

A note in
a cotton field
with blood as evidence
no screams collected
some contorted dream
shaped into transcendence
some obtuse wanting
murdered at the Mason Dixon
some animal instinct on fire
some brutal black sweat
handcuffed to a spiritual
a biting guitar rift
howling a stinky funk
furrowed field
from here to a blood soaked
Mississippi shed
mammy breast feeding
a fat blue-eyed white baby
all innocent and shit

a pot of volcanic grit
competing for the monster
in his trousers
a stylized slave ship
humping the frothy Atlantic
all the way back to Africa
the jazz man held
captive by the noose
the blues man
loaned him
a chaotic rumor about apes
and inferiority sitting inside
Washington's tomb
some marbled artifice
with the names of tribes
stored in the hull of your gut

some fourteen year old accused
of stealing a state, of hiding
from the constitution
found guilty of being human
something in your voice says
all these things
but most of all it says
you are a beautiful
compromise
between

a hurricane and a violin
between an M16
and a feather
between existence
and freshly baked bread.

Small

She says
it was a tiny flutter
she moved her finger
along the line
her heart sang
tears danced down her
face, she felt god move
inside her belly.

Chocolate

She loves chocolate
loves the silky texture
she maneuvers her tongue
through the thin curtain
of sweet milky
dark eyes rolled back
she enjoys this semi
thoughtless indulgence
chocolate yearning
somewhere deep
in the undermost pages
of the suggested middle of her
she gets misty eyed
with a mouth full of chocolate
to contemplate
the fury it took
to convert this orchestra
of flavored sweetness
into this pulsing heaven
someone slowly pounding
a mortar filled with dark goodness
the sucking sound of milk
extraction
the heat and oils produced

divides mind and spirt
the tangy taste of sweat
licked from lips
and savored
soft luscious lips
caught on the cusp
of a sigh
a breath pulled into the lung
then exhaled into the cool
begging mouth
filled with warm milky chocolate.

Fruit and juices

A
pomegranate
between thumb and index
a mango squeezed, just so
gushes thick nectar
between fingers
over knuckles
a bunch of grapes
in the cup
of thick sable hands
produces a monsoon if
the hands are brought to the
mouth
properly caressed
the tongue pressed against
the fruit
juices
will come.

In love & war

There is no mercy in love
only a finite number
of bullets

There is no mercy in war
only a limited number
of resurrections.

Fire

Armed with pens we
go a riding into the sun
bodies filled with riddles
and quoted scriptures
a kicking breathing
glimpse of the orphaned truth
we, orchestras of light
minds cubed from
miles of folded dreams
we dream well
the furniture of our bones
ache for the beautiful terror
for all the unimagined things
to come crashing
into this listless world
our fortunes unknown
yet we cast
reams of light
hoping even a single idea
catches fire.

Motive

My brothers are liars
masked in pomp
their tongues knotted
in serpentine calligraphy
fattened off of absorbed
murders
look in their beds
meaningless whores
we all love the teat
like life support in our mouths
the limo of religion
with its revved engine
waiting to take us to
smog filled heaven
my brothers are
nothing like their dental records
their smiles as sweet as prayers
to sanctify our trek to Hanoi
that crazy lapse of conscience
an oasis to vent
our echoes shore up the disbelief

the tuxedoed president
pitches for the gas company
and its beautiful glass buildings
my generation are
covered in the filth of tradition
they speak and pray and love
and hate the way their ancestors
did
they are good at cloning
their parents
economics has forced
the family nuclear
soon underground
sooner outlawed

we were bred on request
raised in arenas
our lives are a scam
we are paying for
fuck all past and all future
my kind are without hearts
or spines.

Mr. O

8 years of bush doctrine
the world in flames
still they
ask for your papers
like a fugitive slave
the irony
your mamma was born in Kansas
all that terror contained
in the poetry of your smile
they think you uppity
too smart for your own good
they would rather a fool
from the underbelly of Texas
or a man with a mechanical heart
you care too much, sir
love them even when they
spit in the oval

fuckin' up your carpet
imagine what they would
have called you had
your mamma been black
or your father generated
from the soil of South Carolina
they have fed on you for three
years and it has made them schizophrenic

they rant and rave in the streets
they poison their children
the air, the water
starve their parents to hurt you
I see them in the capitol
cutting off their face to spite their nose
all the while you smile
and wish them well.

Book VI

THE WEALTH OF

NATIONS

(2009-2010)

To no end

Luminosity to spare
yet you haggle with idiots
your psychic particulars
sucked until its gardens
are barren

you need a wall
of meticulous heartaches
a spirit of strangled marshes
to keep the vampires at bay

the drugs and liquid fire
are as promising as
the eternal line of ships
that brought your ancestors here

let the world wait
for dreams take time.

Fresh

There is nothing
like a woman
fresh out the shower
painted in sunsets
smelling like satisfaction
and a hand full of lakes.

Men and swords

The men who are remembered aren't
the men who make swords
but the ones who promulgate
their use

the men who use swords are
never smart enough
to understand the minutia
of iron or flesh

when swords are used
flesh is after-thought
scarring is fore

when swords are used
the swing is brutal
the scars are beautiful
the scar is the baby
the swing is the womb.

Flight school

I am here
to teach them how to fly
how to test drive their hearts
to tell them to run
while I put on the shackles
tell them to run in the language
of handcuffs
I am here to tell them
they can make it through the fence
with my back filled with
a lobotomy of bullet wounds
shaped like a college campus
maybe it's the sweet smell
of the chalk
they will use to outline themselves
good morning class
I am here to teach you
how to write your obituary
how to write your eulogy
I was sent by the king
with a mouth full of arrows
here to teach you how to dream
like all your heroes
with their heads chopped off
with their teeth sledge hammered
with their carcasses in museums
with their memories
buried in our garden
of hearts
their machetes
still in their hands.

Enter

She wants me to
slowly sing my way into her
she touched her head and heart, then
said, "enter me through these"
physically?
she said, "yes"
"but how?"
"close your eyes"
I fell apart
coated her skin
then slowly seeped
into all that she was
a quaking occupation
we moved as one
tasted her thoughts
and hummed mosaics through
the halls of her temple.

GOP

Grand Old Party
Grumpy Orwellian Pigs
Got Our Piece
God Over Policy
Giving Out Penis
Gaffe On Par
Got Obama Paranoia
Gaming Other People
Greatest Overpaid Partisan
Governor Oops Perry
Google Overly Patriotic.

Victim

There are no victims
just violated figures
pessimists drinking sorrows
the slum of our beliefs
drifting into irony
she parades as victor
by night, yet blames
the sun for making her a vampire
her teeth and coffin
stained with last night

she makes routine
out of him, yet
assassinations
fill her tomes
her tongue
to razor his name
he claims
she cut his heart out
placed slivers in a blender
while bragging about how heartless
he is

Mephistopheles
perched in their throats
this maddening hum
braised in pointed fingers
crumpled eyes
sermons of beautifully
pious hypocrisy
the victim bribes himself
into thinking god
controls all possibility
all except the one that
tests the boundaries
all except the ones where

we are required to forgive
ourselves.

The handyman

I am a handyman
I do a little of everything
plumbing
gardening
I plug leaks
put up shelves
paint walls
I snake pipes
unclog drains
clean out basements
plow backyards
mow lawns
clean out chimneys
screw in light bulbs
especially in homes
with high ceilings.

Jupiter

She walks in
steps out of her skin
told me she got
magic, a story
a song to open
me right down to
the cell
this calculated freedom
drenched in drums
and soft chords
bass clef
she paused
passed her thumb
over her tongue

eyes rolled back
as she melted into
the mist she created
Orinoko bending the soil
eroding from the pressure
a warm palm consoling
the tropics
a stable cadre of strokes

filled with homemade
explosion
kisses to convince
her nipples they are halos
turned her pagan
in the writhing
grinding
moaning
mouth full
of sermon
licking parables from
the walls of the temple

let us pray

there is no morality
in water
or the sounds we perspire
no morality in an orgasm
that could move god to tears
you are god
there is heaven
in your pleasing.

Bang

Love is fire dreamed
a drawbridge to
blind rage
some vast swan
with knives for breath
love is against logic
survival sometimes
a nostalgic cyclone with
a hand full of rocks
inglorious intent
a wall filled with
splatter marks
zipping ribbons
and piano clangs
an exhausted shepherd
conquering the sheep
tongue of animal
bare bones in
a cryptic flamenco

love will wait for the
moment then
explode within
the faculty of all
things reasonable

love ate the gun
after painting a mural
of the wife and kids
on a beautiful evening
the phonograph needle
as the backdrop
the stage, the lights
the plot
the sucking sound
below the pillow

a final cup of tea
love bangs.

The Art of

There is art in cruelty
the heartless move
with indifference
their faces like stifled horses
trapped in resin
rootless lizard neutrality

there is art in murder
the sucked breath retreats
into the carcass
coils around the things
that need strangling,
the things that say *human*
then returns with a sad
impish grin

there is art in forgetting
a pair of slippers on a balcony
its occupant went flying
his children will rebel against reality
their homes will have
no windows
no railings and most of all
no father.

GOP II

Elephants with short
memories are always an
endangered species.

God

God is trapped in us all
every expression
a way to show us
she is here.

Light

Refracted
through
the spirit prism
bends ignorance
unlocks
primal shrewdness
opens the heart
propels imagination
we are lighthouses
we rip holes
through fog and
dark
we speak consciousness
into minerals
into palms filled with water
we heal with sound
and wind.

Opera

Limbs supple
hewn from holy
fingers press into
the pews
a signature
signed in sighs
sweet tips
to devastate the altar
harmony the carriage
the splashed carnival
of scooped chocolate
struggling through
trembling darkness
the tongue
cross examines
the fingers
slowly tapping
a telegraph
into the marshy
estuary of midnight.

Water

She had water
I was thirsty
now I am drowning.

The devil

The devil is a unique rube
both abolitionist and slaver
constitution and murder
scarlet letter
and purified panic
a well-bred lie
the monstrous precincts
of his eyes are foreign
to love, loves them slowly
his monkey suit covered
in recorded victims
beautiful in the horrors
it disassembles
he is a primal god
his bourgeois enlightenment
as heavy as a century's worth of
transgressions
packed in his crotch
no guilt in his libido
he'll fuck a masterpiece
on the walls of your
terminus
satan the pulpit and
devour your senses
dislocate his melancholy
in your spread wings
will leave fire
and glory
and pleasure

the flapping sounds
sexual under his nail
the casualties of his vocabulary
enjoys the bloodletting
the disasters he
breeds

to inherit his swag
is to be a creature
of deception.

Lil Kim

Daddy was a scream
willing to turn a city into
a glass museum
his senile pompadour
a metaphor for
all his intangibles
he was much smaller
than he appeared
the implications
will quicken the blood
the turmoil in his Dior glasses
says it all
how does one sell
a nuclear age
to a starving man?
pave the street with
grumbling bellies
erect statues
of a machine gun
drinking a glass of wine
write a suicide note
for every suicide note
kill the wounded
before they get wounded
dear Lil Kim
daddy was a scream
you, you can be a song.

Zanzibar 1563

You are poetry
golden limbs and liquid locks
how many centuries
have we wasted dancing
circles in the blackness
the felony of touching
your temple has turned
me to stone
solid rock, granite
trembling brick

the sweet
peach flavored
corridors
worked until divinity
is splashed in creamy shapes
skin like glowing embers
drunk off the light

we squeezed into another
dimension
our loins doubled as heaven
the ceiling fan
a mystic whispering
turning slowly
and inside the quaking quiver
of the back-stroke
you looked back
saw that smirk
licked your lips
knowing I would
be in this pulpit all night.

Truth

The creators of truth
will never admit
that truth does not exist
only vacant spaces
for the invented we
we are all invented
we could be ants
or art work
or needles
all imagined things
a point where
life and light bends
and chaos
come a skipping
through the blackest
of codes
we breathe new
experiences into the static
universe
our throats like cannons
for the darkness
perch for hulking vultures
we preach the lips until
wood splint
until there is no moon
no night to open us
we trade ideas until we are
serene, until silence
is the only language we know.

The grave

The grave
is a metaphor
a post-it note
of all the things we
have not done
a poster child
fluent in forever
the grave
does not call
or summon
it simply waits.

Distance

She is tapped into my psyche
she hears my thoughts
from a thousand
miles away
manufactures my dreams
and places them in
my head
she falls me
in and out of
earthly love

I love her
there is no time
between us
no space
no exist
we just are
the way we are
she's run off with
princes and kings
in numerous lives
I have married her
closest friend and
ran with her heart
in my quiver
I have died in wars
for her honor
she has visited the stake
treasoned her king
her country
set ships at sea on fire
for the love between
made love while falling into
a den of lions
we've been lion and hunter
her and I

I have stalked her
she has stalked me
I ended up on her plate
she ended up
in my stew
and every time

the words are the same
the feeling
the taste
the nostalgia
sepia and orange
a billion years old
micro macro curled
into one big bang
it's the dark matter
a billion years in a
billionth of a second
just a thought
a feeling
savor her on the tongue
her aroma dancing through
my olfactory
right into the brain stem
the flash
the calm
her eyes
the universe spinning
around her
swollen belly
the storm she carries
is more than
we can both bare
eternity
is an arrow with no bow
shot into the dark
vacuum
of the universe.

Magic

These is no magic
only a way of seeing
look at the rain fall.

Abstract

The dance
two figures in the snow
a sky the color
of the ocean captured
in a jar
oil perception
a muted horn
ceiling, broken floor
calm fire kindled
a house
white rectangular heart
black divide
the memory of the fading
it fades
and we pause to
pick up the pieces.

NC

North Carolina
every day I think of your
dark damp soil, the
rustics of your rural
Americana
Carolina
our destinies are a
religion amongst the gods
beautiful atoms of night
extracted from the
terror of eternity.

Hmmm

Your chaos is pragmatic
the secret architecture
of your spine
moves the land
the land bequeaths
huddled sonics
sultry sounds
brain moans
speak volumes
pages, exposed
to the haiku of your lap
a labyrinth of prose
passing over
a trained tongue
oceans me in
gorgon of tilted hips
black grace of lust
prayed into the skin
sucked like enslaved salt
the quotient of our love
blooms a thousand
infinities
I'll feed you moans
for breakfast
dick for lunch
oil slicked floors
sticky with infidelity
fallen flags and broken heart
bent spears hollowed
out with godlike panting
your oasis grasping the water's edge
breathless you heal
my compliment of wounds
my scars ennobled
in the myth of you
glory in the girth

eyes rolled teeth marked
lips magnificent
surrender yes
I will fuck the numerals
out of your social security number
dare me
destroy me lover
with your primal heaven
with the liquid
algorithms of your crotch.

Meaning

Words are aircrafts
carried by an invisible
intangible thing
they soar but
when they crash
devastating.

The Gut

Tested love
frozen unbelievable love
quiet empty bedded love
it will gut you
but the feeling is beautiful.

Man

Man rhymes with murder
just thought you should know
men sell hell
cannon balls
and fire songs
and pleading nooses
and blood filled coffins
our hearts are angled
hear the apocalypse
jumping inside our bellies
we get lonely too
get trapped by the silence
so we scream at the world
choking back the
guitar's twang
the weaponry
of our hearts
sharpened by the terrors
of our shredded youth

men are graveyards
roaming through a
an abandoned city
we manipulate
our way into things
and amputate the things
we can't carry
we are efficient funerals
stuffing the pain
into sandwich bags
eating our way through the
things that hurt us most

men are gentle
gentle creatures
fragile beings

this storming, grinding
rage
is the sound of our bodies
denying the fact that
we are human.

Time

Nostalgia
blinds us
time takes
the scales away
leaves us a full
song or sermon
those who conserve
culture are fools
imagine time held captive
moving forward
is no option
weighted steps
ironic twists
eventually we'll be thrashing
against a world
where we are fossils
under the dusty palm
of time.

NYE

After
the ball drops
and the blurry room
tightens around your head
when the alcohol
stops rattling your spirit
the weed smoke leaves you
in an ocean of abstractions
breathe easy knowing
the world ends in a few.

Book VII

THE BOOK OF FORMS

(2008-2009)

Poet

You struggle with
pen and language
you eat books
bed ideas
tear into the raw
guts of theories

poet
you struggle with
hue and tone
color and line
and composition
you grab meaning
by its throat
your knife like eyes
pealing back the layers

poet
your very walk is choreography
there is muse about you
your posture
graced subtle marvel
you have worked
those feet till
the bone was blood
and the blood was holy

poet
it's not the language
we love
it's your pause
the slightest
twist in your oratory
your body, your word
a simple piece of art
this finite act of bravery

held so high
so beautifully
so honest
tears are insufficient

poet
you inspire
not because of anything
you have created
but by the fact
of who you are.

Poem for artist

We had to bite
the universe in thirds
to stay alive
to catch breath
we sang
danced
clapped
and plastered
the segregated self
in temples
in back alleys
dressed
in undecipherable darkness
we are the opera house
that swallowed the richter
we are earthquakes
we dream in miracles
and hidden silences
in coded thunder
and higher nightmares
in metaphysical melodies
and spellbinding fevers
of the illuminated psyche

we dream
in struggle shaped parables
and blood blazed narratives
of brimstone
there she goes
dreaming in continents again
we are the anti-dream awake
we conjure sorcerers
crazy
screaming
at the world
because sometimes

screaming
is all we can do

languaging
ourselves into being
we are paradoxes
perched on half tragedies
a frankenstein of the past
400 years zeused together
snatched seventh
speaking in tongues
for we are Oba's children

we hack our way into
the veins of fiends
and return pluralized
mutilated yes
we deconstruct
the unclenched wires
of exploded hearts
and eulogize the dreams
of our lost fathers
eyes glossed over
looking at a distant son
a gone father
the future in stalemate
only photos
of an uncrowned madness
the sun leaking through
his fingers
don't lose the son
it is the only light we know
but it is hard to speak
when your breath is flint
and the world
is gun powder
poet
never be silent.

God and gold

Caught by
the beautiful art of
unsheathing swords
a conundrum of our crimes
frozen in stone
holy Siddhartha's bosoms
split by the fearless calligraphy
of covert sycamores
swooping down
swallowing cities
accused brandished pupils
jammed in a semi-automatic gaze
no fear just eyes
balled up
clenched down
filled with static fury
with the scientific silence
that makes us monsters

imagine Billie in a Berlin
church howling
Einstein's theories
chalked up inside her throat
the blade of darkest christendom
with all its chariots aflame
with ten thousand B52s
carrying the mechanized
apocalypse across the galvanized sky
what of all the conjugated
niggers
gooks
spicks
fags
and all the dark bastards
who fuck their meaning away
who breed

to the cadence
of the industrial revolution
those born to be loaded into pistons
into the romanced wing
of avant-garde murder
see Ginsberg and Baraka
Lorca and Kaufman
Dali and Basquiat
in their prudent denial
in the basement hopped up
on the modernist trauma
their communist faces like
jade antelopes at dawn

have you seen Miles
his horn pointed toward god
toward the madrasas of Harvard
as if philosophy
could transmute Murdoch
out fox him
his grave covered in
smoke shawls of
sub-atomic cruelty
the collected sciences
the drug dress
the amnesia cavity of
pre-recorded clowns
exposé of the deprived half self

oh heavens
tumble swift
beneath this gentle hammer
of cremated prayers
stratified monk bone
sky kisser
son of mighty black Zeus
scooped from Osiris' rib
from the spell caster's manual
lovers of words and stone

of graves and silent candles
of hidden faces canonized
in imperial burning heaven
a rotating sepulcher
of civilized nooses
of computerized
and radiant death
geometric temples for
the robotic gods of
symmetrical darkness

star filled cycles of scary
moonless wanting
shoved up against
the callous braying organ
of betrayed physics
artificial love
kneeling brutal neophyte
bullshit of Rome and New York
see the gas chamber
whispering numerical poems
into the great cabal
of blue exalted neon
whiteness preaching
raining choirs of tyrannical
tambourines in their hot sweaty
truncated dreams
calling across the chasm
Africa's children
coniggerated
in their codified kidnappings
doused in their gentrified truths
calling out to mighty black Zeus.

Old man (for John McCain)

Where is your whale
your neutered colossus
meticulously un-sexed
your borrowed narratives
of prison camps
that amputated your morals
liquefied your conscience
drained it grudgingly from
the lips of the sound barrier
as if Cambodia or Vietnam
came roaring
into your living room
declared itself hero
war heads carrying roses
through the poppy fields
through the killing fields
through fields of scrambled minds
singing
songs of the strategically
invisible

eyes and limbs
like a patchwork of
enlightened scars
french-kissing
the sub-urban sprawl
falling in love
with the killing machine
these sanitized tombs
telegraphing this
oblique blindness of ours
this re-assembled truth
re-lapsed god
our sons in theaters of war
re-casted in camouflage
the shrill winds screaming

through their designer interiors
covered in blue murder
storming the beaches of heaven

old man
was it something your father said
that sent you
somersaulting toward
this staged calamity
the streets of your amnesia
necromanced with shiny
napalm rain
post-visible with
promises to uncork
the apocalypse, twice
as if you could re-bottle the sons
of yesterday

old man put the orchestra down
this symphony of clattering hooves
as if the devil himself
breast fed you metal flavored darkness
callous the days that lay
beneath your microscope
scalpel
old man you've crafted an
eloquent tragedy
light
a labyrinth of skilled carpentry
a quantum circus abandoned
in the woods of our prayers
old man
we are all part glass
fragile vulnerable tapestries
of fiction
look out across the ocean
can't you hear Beethoven
in the waves
can't you see the markings of all

our invented gods
have you ever tasted
the smell of freshly baked bread
walking through the fortress
of your lungs
have you ever
cradled your heart
held it out toward the theater
of stars and marveled
at this beautifully
brutal continuum
this eternal manuscript of silence
let go old man
let go
of the dogma of fools
scrape the numerical lust
from your face
and dream of a day when
our children won't have to parachute
down the barrels of machine guns
old man.

Dynamite ministers

To the dynamite ministers
cerulean echoes
from the catacombs
of Rome
to the blood metallic
without cause or reason
without mouth or refracted light
lobbied merchants of
consolidated distraction
doing the Rowe v Wade
Karl Rove on his breath
dreaming dreams
to un-exist you

masters of the mediocre science
enemies of the darker ones
memorizing launch codes
smells like Third Reich
deregulated patriotism
choose a country
name it beauty queen
call it Alaska
or statutory rape
trigonometry at its best
the no look hand off
the baby head fake
screw stem cell research
he'll clone the imagination

the final frontier
is satellite assisted group think
deputize it teleprompter
let us pray for a H-bomb
with a higher IQ
and pretend John McCain
ain't art deco small pox

some postmodern slave ship
gone republican
they'll copyright god
patent death
doctor the packaging
side step the truth
with its amputated limbs
at Walter Reid
so they could franchise
the sun and email earthquakes
to countries we don't like

how about a Bible for a brain
a corporation for a heart
just scale back on the dreaming
we'll Paris Hilton and
good morning Vietnam
our way back into the White House
paint it oilfield
inaugurate it Black Water
some hip hop version
of the polio vaccine
something to make you nod
call it heroine
purple haze
Afghanistonian apocalypse
shock and awe for moose

the American way
wearing prison camp
label it Guantanamo
call it Wall Street
feed it Pentagon
feed it hawk
and neo-con
and negro-phobia
feed it commercial free paranoia
a splash of bullshit
let it cook

e-bay it back to Hitler
call it fox
the murder house
Eichmann and Goebbels
in Prada
call her John the Baptist
with a semi-automatic
abortion clinic strapped
to her back
call it the war department
the old boy network
reform in uniform
as if our children die in third person
for statutes unconstitutional
who will analyze their grave stones
or un-devil the skies over Oklahoma
where is the flag
when you need it most
where are the ballot boxes
not manufactured by Halliburton.

For Elaiwe

Mama's breast milk
must have been
a baptist church
a molotov cocktail
with eyes like
a practiced suicide
what delectable slice
of heaven did
father articulate
into her being
must have called
her Jezebel
or Magdalene

did you practice
being invisible
in that language of his
I can see him now
lying to himself
saying he is dark enough
to slow down time
her neon happiness
skipping through
the armageddon of
his limestone heart
aerodynamiced you be
functioned you from notion
from dark columns
of negroness
from books
and theoretical
absence
be it as
thus it be
you a captive of
unexploded meaning

308

in retrospect
this is not moon
not love
just lonely girls
at a heart parade
congratulating
themselves

go find Malcolm
in your catalogue of dreams
tell him he was wrong
tell him there is no god
there is no heart
no hope
when
memory fails
the greatest of saints
tell him, take his Bible
back to Mecca
feed it to that black stone
her face painted forgive
her ears removed
arms akimbo
lips to the sky

you are a song
that never repeats.

Brooklyn

Brooklyn
his dreams chauffeured
inside cherry blossoms
smile and teeth like
New Orleans 1849
sky ripe smell
cotton barges
hauling history across rivers
the darkest corners
of commerce
calculating the
agony of sunlight
mutated Africaness
the time, the distance
the sepia breed
nightmare tongue
carved from
negative enlightenment
still, your face gentle
like you had
god over for tea
bone white polyester
stiff with controlled chaos
powder blue suede
brotha who are you
this photo lies
we could have been kin
lies
photo this
you are who?
brotha suede blue
powder chaos controlled
with stiff polyester
white bone tea
for over god
had you?

like gentle
face your still enlightenment
negative from carved tongue
nightmare breed
sepia the distance
the time
the Africaness mutated
sunlight of agony
the calculating commerce
of corners
the darkest
rivers across history
hauling barges
cotton smell
ripe sky
1849 New Orleans
like teeth and smile
blossoms cherry inside
chauffeured dreams
his
Brooklyn.

Leaving

No
obvious hidden
meaning
nothing more
less her
his lost
found real fake
filled?
empty?
Yes.

Touch

Body doused in sticky
a million microscopic nipples
fanned out across her arms
the delicate muscle tightens
the economy of sweat
sweet darkness
the perspiration breathes
slightly open
the body curls scientific
slightly open
she presses the
pleading flesh
no words
just hot tongues
twirling atomic circles
wrestling that freaky
molecular madness
from the velvety trembling
erogenous pacing slow
the body curls scientific
cherished wood
the perspiration breathes
extracting metaphor
from vibrating timpani
humming internal
sprawled soil
no Nietzsche
no Spinoza
just pleasure swelling
fingers gentle along the sanctum
the body curls scientific
steady myth beneath
betwixt the inner thighs
sweet darkness
the keys pushed all the way in
the cooing fortress

throbs and pulsates
and screams this dirge
flesh extended
beyond reason
the body curls scientific
halos broken
raw carnal
tremors that split
spines open, arched
legs spread, just so
the economy of sweat
the core spills religious
fevered lusty
chords weeping
sacred between her teeth
as Ovid whispers Rome
into her gentle bristles
the body curls scientific
she eases into the explosion
rides it to the cusp
and rolls the balled up energy
around inside her cheeks
face suffocating the darkness
clasping the thousandth degree
factored, squared, uglied
the delicate muscle tightens
arithmeticed until
she's ignited sky
dreams aflame
the body curls scientific
mouths filled with holy elixir
the silence swallowed
the tongue gallops
babbles, sexual, ecstatic
in raptured blindness
chest open
like tomorrow's impossible
like now is never
the body exhales

to the point of fabricated death
the body curls scientific
fanned out across her arms
a million microscopic nipples.

GW Bush

Evening lights his theme park face
lost in childlike marvel
nearly swallowed the silver spoon
curious George cloaked in lunatic
ego times empire equals empire
easing through divinity's tube
hand him Lady Macbeth
her eyes and breath
godless
this kamikaze Bible gang

oil slicked bravado
atomic paranoia
Halliburton
deity of the oil field
our president is fluent in Texaco
he speaks Exxon well
his goons singing
a military love song
chorus mostly
chaos mostly
no magic.

Black genius

We know of kings
who carried greatness
like flowers at funerals
who wore lunch counters
like Jim Crow was self-imposed
silence, was meditation
our sanity, the transposed art
brutal tool shed, perched
inside our fathers throats
bitter songs of flying
back to heaven
a future sculpted from
a marvelous turmoil
phrased on legal papers
our insurrected faces
chattering with visions
accused of breathing
of magnetic blackness
of hiding continents
in our dreams, these
the beautiful children
in their monstrous skin
triumphant
in their jeweled sleep

they speak as if she
was some unlucky whore
wearing Lincoln's cod piece
Madison weaved into her speech
segregated slices of the south
served at her abortion party

so they fly the flag
of the hate they love
the contradiction sentenced
to contradict itself

I wonder did Jefferson
blacken up before he raped her
ever so gently
did they lay on their backs
looking up at the stars
lost in conversation
her fingers running idly through
the gardens of his trousers
stained with cherry blossoms
his curated terror, dreaming inside
her vulgar labyrinth of womb
our mothers, daughters
lynched with genetic nooses

Nat Turner must have been
Benjamin Banaker's father
his big black boom-box
heart pressed up against
dashiki-ed Washington
Osiris-ed him in secret, no
the perfect black
Egypting the blueprints
brought Giza to the Potomac
chopped into thirteen pieces
chess board colonies
a pyramid
South Carolina
smells like the Congo
broke the language
reconstructed Osiris' penis
pre-reconstruction
planted it in Washington
the tallest building
Banaker, confederate African

King's greatness
funeral counter
imposed meditation
art perched throats flying

heaven from turmoil papers
faces, visions breathing blackness
continents, these children
skin triumphant
sleep she whore
piece speech
south party flag
love sentenced itself
Jefferson her gently
backs
stars
conversation through trousers
blossoms in womb
daughters
noose been
father boom-box
against Washington
no black prints
Potomac pieces
pyramid
South Carolina
Congo language
penis reconstructed
Washington building
African.

Honey limbs

Jars of midnight hips
flesh, tangy
like a mouth full of
copper coins flying
believers tongue massages
the ripe aroma
exploding sun
trumpet meets drum
levitated mini-skirt
a nameless wanting
climbing into the g-spot
salty syrius pouring
swollen moans into the gentle
rippled center, lap rousing
core of premeditated gravity
every stroke of the clock
calculated beautifully knotted
executed warm
oils, breath, music
pushed into flesh
orchid filled with sap harmonizing
moving slippery memories
the milk of dawn smeared
spilled

blooming sunsets
supernova sweaty
godlike spoons
of bottled screams
exploded erratic
paint splashed collage
symphonic
the edges pushed back
crying
the curved earth
the hefty hypotenuse

320

sweeter than morning
the secret religion gyrating
tendered through tongues
intense melodies of muscles speaking
organs pressed
into circles of finite decadence
sorcerers funk
moon juice kinky
whiskey with
jars of midnight hips
the forest damp
with the pilgrimage
of spent instruments
deep in deconstructed silence.

Your tube

Television
equalizes
evens the field
makes idiots
of everyone.

Dual

She be
waiting on god
he be busy with
mothers of the ghetto steps
full throttle aria, lip turned up
her dynamite eyes and plinth of face

suggests she is holding the messiah for ransom

halo of monarchs perpetually circle her crown
this brick building, her personal metaphor
no weather divides her light
imagines her painted future
seeds all grown
shining thus.

Saint Brooklyn

Your stadium of heart
quartered in love's apartment
stacked with holy books
voice pressed against
the ceiling of your youth
where are your children
your stadium of heart
to graze on shards of blindness
isolated sheep, calling out to
a flock of shepherds
hungry for the sufferer's power
raw cryptic illumination
Brooklyn is a city of churches
a junction of screaming prophets
quartered in love's apartment
your heart left homeless
their agency distorted
what truth anchored in sweat
bleeds you
what song chained in commotion
of chest speaks
be it the many, the few to save
stacked with holy books
when your empire falls
what of your inner
beautiful jigsaw of tongue
unfinished face rounded
boneless voice gashing
entourage, carrying centuries of
doctored Nazareth
voice pressed against
frightened by what you'll become
coded scriptures
against your silent, dark blue
your love is terrifying
as if you have swallowed

the madness of realms unknown
saint of measured sunshine
the ceiling of your youth
jealous of your belief
memorized heaven
in this chaos
your sorcery is meaningless
yet, I am jealous of your belief
frightened by what you'll become
when your empire falls
your heart left homeless
to graze on shards of blindness.

Yusef (for Yusef Komunyakaa)

The terror
sits beautiful
in your mouth
oh, the alchemy you are made of
calamity you have translated
from embers to monarchs
the dark silences
vanquished by sweet singing
holy the eyes
the truth they must have seen
the devil in his finest raiment
smoking, dreams on the battlefield
the trek through sterile psychosis
through altered Vietnam
I saw it happen on your face
the carbine floating
metal spirits of friends
turned sheets of chaos
saw them roll onto the floor
the muscles of your lived face relaxed
into the subtle exposure
as you stuffed your head into
the cannon's mouth
crawled into the timeless
opening in our heads
these are your scars
trying to save an already dead man
Yusef, there is no
guilt in observation
you remind me of Hersschell
such beauty
of Ngoma, noble still
I have never touched that wall
never want to touch that wall
the grass whispering
through the reflected ink

the blade of the gun ship
beating its pre-planned course
I hope this world is not that blade
your heart not gun ship
your love is our
greatest miracle
truth is, you could
have been a monster
but you chose this beauty.

Blue

Guitar turned time machine
magician's black hole
shaman spaceship
collapse-blue
backwoods
mississippi madman
swamp sound
medicine
holy lucifer's
sonic gospel axe
bleeder's anthem is
pray us heaven is
always
god us forward
bend the portal
carriers of darkest now
stomp a tune through
smoke, ancestor us here
calabash grenade
primate language
chatter, mumble, groan
deposit painted grief
burning corners, yes
silent
raptured trembling
Alabama be
Congo too
vivid dreams
splitting rooms
light bulbs wrestling history
exhausted nightmares
sing Abe Lincoln beautiful
Orisha house
Shango guarded
temple
un-mammaled

instruments disappearing
buckets accumulating
shipwreck, shipwreck
stinky hallelujah floor
fathered ritual
history
fattened
ships, ships
drugged flesh
haunting dangerous patterns
configured land
beautiful noose
accidental yearning
unlikely
simple
free.

Transcribed lost

The surgeon's knife
is beautiful
baffling science kneeling
into the womb
of psychosis

is it genocide
if nobody dies?
when spliced, does the molecule
become a different empire?
does a heart still love
between silences
after the prophet's blade?

it hugs the flesh
of shiny replica gods
reprograms their discomfort
casually strolling off into
a small corner.

Goddess of

She stepped
out of an octave
octagons drawn
tribe eyes
melodic brown
black metal stand still
pause of ripened flesh
framed against a
frozen masquerade
the illuminated financiers
nightmare merchants
peddlers of the impossible ain't
flames caged in the
language of their
bartered
eternal
fictitious
commodity

tiny satellites of self
scattered behind her
dreamlike walk
pulling eons of conversations
prolonged prayers
colonized monopolies of
expired greatness
dreadful
beautiful for
reasons known and unknown
trailed by a bewitched
narrative of cloth
whispering spheres and
realms of poetry.

Michael

Magi of the moonwalk
you must have inherited
your heart, your love
from the chest of a supernova
through veins of a miracle

saw you carry the
light and chaos
the love and hopes
of an entire generation
in a single
gloved hand
glittering
carrying galaxies
Michael
I have seen you
slowed time
seen you shape-shift
your way into the psyche
of millions

singing songs
to save the children
to heal the world
but I wonder, Michael
I wonder
In the quiet moments
when you are alone
away from the flashing cameras
what really moved your heart
what really pressed your thoughts
Michael?

and in my dreaming head
I see you sitting
with Deepak

reading poems by Rumi
and you are shining Michael

you are shining
and you are beautiful
beautiful
as you have always been.

Palestine

I see you with your
bare hands
with your disaster of heart
believing
with your shattered
blood sweetened teeth
organs on parade
like a photo finish
your quarantined hatred
out of context on CNN

I see you
outside of this religion
this country
this skin you claim
I see you Palestine
with no Muhammed
no Balfour
no Zionist
no Naser
no Yaser
no West
no Bank
no Gaza
no atom divided yes

I see you
with your Jerusalem shaped heart
Koran eyes
throwing rocks
at a concept
little boys should never be
homeless in a land full of rocks
in a world too brutal
for the concocted terrors
of your dreams

I know you are dreaming
you are dreaming of cornfields in Kansas
of racing the wind
on an open plain
because you've seen it in their movies
so you dream of horses
and bright lights
and fast cars
and John Wayne
so you wear your favorite nike
t-shirt to throw rocks
at tanks
centuries crashing into your lungs
why are you screaming at the trees
Palestine
clawing the dust
Is it because you too are invisible
hoping your screams
will grant you visibility
chewing your way through
the wailing wall

what bravery
those bare hands
a rock, your heart
versus all their collected sciences
of metal and doom
what drives you, Palestine
do you even think you can win

when these men
will bring armageddon to the wombs
of your women
what of your shouts
when they own your language
when they possess bombs bigger
than your god
Palestine

I too know humiliation
I know how it feels
when Israel
clutches her purse
and walks to the other side
white phosphorus
like a brutal exodus across the sky
Daliesque
you are only a fraction
barely human
how dear you be
when they have spent
billions devising schemes
to slaughter your dreams
Palestine
give in
please
walk away
surrender
for there is no
climbing into the throat
of a tank to reason
with the artillery
for chances are
we are alive simply
because our lungs
are dreaming of breath
our hearts are dreaming
of moving blood
so surrender
walk away
or strap
a thousand pounds
of roses to your chest
and run into the nearest mall
and hug every single
human being
you find
love them with all you are made of

336

because it is your love
that they fear most.

Book VIII

BLACK ANGELS WITH SKY BLUE FEATHERS

(1996-1999)

A rose in Harlem

There is a rose in Harlem
with twigs in her eyes
twisting her tongue
talking candles
photographing her ovaries
on my essence
she prayed in French whispers
with baby angels pouring
libations on her nipples
spelling children
in a Cuban dialect
blowing eternities
through African villages
filled with bamboo songs

I once had a glimpse of her wings
calling...
my melanin collect
with seventeen syllable movements
her kisses were in braille
her eyes braided across my shadows
she had soft speaking feathers
sprouting from her belly button
holding twelve sticks of
Japanese incense
burning star maps in her womb
her past lives swung
from her second self
tightly wrapped in maroon roses
she took baths in the moon's eyeshadow
washing away the scars
of her addiction
...to love

there is a rose in Harlem
rocking a Sudanese fro
her thoughts
crocheted in her eyes
with a halo the size
of Nairobi
and you can't help but imagine
damn!
is that god I taste on your tongue?
her lips were like touches
from a black butterfly's clef note
she spoke in uranium orgasms
with nipples
the size of quarters
with valleys on their tips
my tongue tying twilights in her mind
moving mountains
between her memories
I'd spend ten eternities in jail
to have her photographed in braille
give me my eyes
I'd wear her scent for a thousand years...
bypass god
and send her my prayers
myself.

In these parts

In these parts they say
even shadows cry
walls sing sad songs
and sinister sidewalks ask why
shackled in fear we live in filth
mentally raped
and them bathing in their guilt
we drift in this limbo-like place
where it hurts to smile
we pray to die
partying all night making callous attempts
to drink our blues away
numbing our souls to a pain
we can't help but feel.

My shadows

My story will be told
in an ancient Chinese tongue
some hybrid morse code
mummy language
tap dancing my shadows in technicolor
slapping fives with light
to catch the echoes of harsh realities
scribbling Nat Turner's name
in calligraphy
on the backs of city roaches

my shadows come in the form
of cannabis smoke
teleporting messages
from souls on sunken slave ships
doing hyperbola flips
on sacred temple walls
decoding a billion slave beatings
throwing revolutionary
meetings in light bulbs
writing sheet music to silent songs
sung by Somali sistas
with fiber optic afros
swinging from nooses
made of Bible sheets
explaining scriptures
to unborn fetuses

my shadows come in the form
of wide-hipped Zulu women
who cornrow hieroglyphics
in their pubic hairs

challenging god
to immaculate conception matches
bearing messiahs in ink blotches
tattooing the names of
African elephants
under the armpits
of Shaolin monks
meditating to lava lamps

so my story will be told
in the language of shadows
shadows that fist fight reality
to maintain their sanity
in small glass jars like goldfish
my shadows play guitars
with no strings
hanging themselves
to prove there is
life after death

I see my shadows all the time
in the subways and on sidewalks
begging for change
but... you... you give them money
because you're listening with your eyes
they are begging for change
with scriptures stitched in their palms
dragging bags of ancestral bones

Amadou Diallo was shot 19 times
because his fingerprints
were the same as Nat Turner's
so take a look at your fingerprints
and tell me...
who do you see?

because they walk amongst us
with afros shaped like cowrie shells
crucifixes branded on their lips
yet they speak not of god...

only of revolution
telling stories
of how they jumped off slave boats
destined to unify their souls
under water to form icebergs
and candles
to light our way back home...

the sinking of the Titanic
was no accident
that was us
and they know it
why do you think
they are so afraid of the 13th floor
because 13 times 2
plus 13 divided by 2 equals infinity
and they can't take that
away from us.

16

Her face
plastered with war paint
that form trenches
through which armies
of her insecurities marched
wearing camouflaged suits
and tear gas mascara
masking behind navy blue eyelids
covering concrete eyes
in concrete jungles
laying in pain...
humming stories of
seven mispronounced spaces
seven misunderstood lives
that live their deaths in tin cups
strangling her silence
scrawling her father's
name on her eyeballs
trying to understand his pain
that bled from her blue skin
cosmologically cosmetic cause
she was only sixteen
and naïve... so...
she traded eternity
for a nickel bag
smoking away her pain
pulling daddy's hands
out of her draws
in her face I saw
the three unmentioned
dimensions of self
that expose
the exoskeleton of exegists
that exist in eggshells in Egypt
she wore blood colored

lipstick as a reminder
trying eloquently to explain
the oprobrity
of her daddy's
epidermal superficiality
he was only
skin deep
experimenting on her ego
cutting away small slices of her
hiding himself inside her
... he hid
so schizophrenia
became her pastime
she jumped in and out
of beds like personalities
acquiring, multiplying
her personalities
so that it would be difficult
to find her true self.

A junkie's banter

I speak in artifacts
with museums
in my bloodstream
during slavery I was
teaching tae-bo and ebonics
I've got mummies
on my payroll
pawning pyramids
and collecting
government checks
perspiring ankhs
and snorting motherships
I get flashbacks of forever
because I am forever
these shackles can't hold me

I sold wings to slave ships
with scarabs running
around inside my lungs
doing the macarena
and practicing black magic like
life got me hanging
by my metro card
meeting deadlines
jobs don't free us
in this race against time
we need space
but they don't know
what time it is
so they're spaced out

I'm anti clock
spray painting roaches

and kidnapping
martian butterflies
with speech impediments
holding them hostage
trying to get that feeling
that feeling of angels
flying around inside my head
heading nowhere slow

this is me
breaking the rules
like bony blonde
haired while girls
from Omaha Nebraska
with entire African tribes
swimming in their pelvis
freeing themselves
from what they hate most
about this country

where possession of melanin
is a misdemeanor
in New York
it is punishable by death
in California
you can get a good caning
if you are caught with more than
light dosages
ask Rodney...
he has cars as proof
proof that these people
need to change their thinking
think yourself a new mind

stand up for something
be a lesbian today

a revolutionary tomorrow
try prostitution
be a vegetarian...
and starve yourself to death
because guess what
even the trees
eat animals.

I don't know

Sometimes I ride the trains
for seven or eight days
straight, or in circles
trying to figure out
who I was in my next life
I keep getting this
strange feeling that
this girl I'm seeing...
is me in my next life
come back to this time
trying to figure me out
so that next time around
life won't be so crazy for me
but the thing is,
she has no recollection
of ever being me
and I do not remember
ever being her
because chances are
I am her in her next life
come to this lifetime
trying to figure her out
so that next time around
life won't be so crazy for her
or me or her or me
if there were no clocks
and no calendars
where in time would we be?

Untitled

She had time-torn ravines
on her face
with tangerine ravens
flying mud cloth patterns
through her sanity
leaving lava droppings
on her soul
burning holes
in her madness
calling Coltrane
blowing blood stained sheets
out of numb nostrils
bleeding blindfolds
each eye stitched shut
with white
hypodermic needles

she said god
was dancing in her veins
twisting himself into
infinity signs
singing
Hebrew hymns
in a raspy Irish brogue
poisoning her sanity
killing her self
esteem

she painted
her prom dress red
as a tribute to her late uncle
the one she murdered
in his sleep

for raping her dreams
constantly powdering her face
trying to lift his fingerprints
from her birth canal

she had indigo tears of joy
laughing herself to misery
lying about the many lives
she lived
driving stakes in the coffins
of vampires
who seeded her
coughing blood smoke
her eyelashes beat-boxing
in couture
feather dancing kisses
in her eyes
throwing block parties
in her womb
ten dollars at the door
all you can eat
and they came in
by the thousands

riding her rhythm
searching for her heart beat
which she had,
candy wrapped
in barbed wire

zombie dancing
with potential messiahs
to violin drumbeats
that beat her
heartbeat to death

to raise it from the dead
and beat it to death again
she relived her past lives
so many times
not realizing
so now she sings
sad songs
waiting for the day
when she can cry in peace.

Underwaterstanding

My metaphors count
from one to amphibian
Zulu-spitting
dolphins with ponytails
and cell phones
making calls
to a land fish
who has forgotten
how to breathe
under water

we have lost
our under water
standing on land
amphibians
who swim in the blues
the great blue
see
we have lost our eyes
so we became cell-fish
labeled jail-bait
I have lost my gills
so yes I am guilty
guilty of strangling
the rest of me
in a bowl of
chocolate milk

I was told
I am too subliminal
to be understood
standing

so now I sit
and recite
in the subways
on sub-waves
thinking until
my thought
sprained its ankle

I was my
grandmother's eulogy
stitched under
my father's tongue
planted in the ear
of my mother
in the ears of
most folks
taking them to places
where geese lay
light bulbs in
foreign languages
and lavender skies
rain scented candles
on the bare backs
of Celtic surfs
trapped in triangular
sun dials
mimicking mummies
with Marley locks
mud stomping
Cantonese calligraphy
on pyramid ceilings
sealing in cemented souls
booby trapped in flesh
I have seen
a blind man look
for meaning in life

what are you looking for?

Clay jars

I saw a sista
this morning
growing out of a tree
searching for her roots
picking up pieces
of what was left
of what was right
about her
she had heroin
flavored grease
doing the shuffle
on her scalp
with varicose veins
in her eyes
shining like those
fifty cent pieces
they had in Jamaica
when I was a boy
she had slave trail
stretch marks
where her smiles
used to be
said she finally
caught on to
what was going on
inside her head
had too many needs
filling them with needles
running around
basing blindly
sex was the disease
that cured her
loneliness

and on lonely nights
you could hear her
crawling through
the pipes
screaming in
forgotten whispers
in that moment
she was super human
half woman
half cocaine tears
burning tribal scars
on her cheeks
she was in a hurry
she was in a hurricane
blowing her way
to her next fix
bedding
ghetto merchants
carrying suitcases
packed with HIV
and WIC checks

she had a clay jar
filled with sand
keeping count of
her miscellaneous
abortions
the ones she wanted
to remember
she wanted to
remember
that she wanted
to have babies
to hold in her arms
against her withering
youth

but they kept
slipping through
the cracks in her lips
falling into this jar
this jar
she wanted to drop
so bad
but holding it
had also become a habit
so she rocks
her clay jar
to sleep
hush little baby
hush.

My grandmother

My grandmother was
a bowlegged
Japanese lesbian
with orange hair
bleeding zodiac signs
in darkness
humming
suicidal scriptures
in telepathic languages
forming triangular moons
out of voodoo dolls
building ice castles
in her heart
laying down
her thoughts
on train tracks
to be crucified by sanity

her bloodshot eyes
tip toed on
micro wave smoke
singing ghettoes
in between blinks
sipping blue liquids
out of Nigerian crystals
to spell Billie Holiday's name
backwards
on all 27 dimensions
of herself falling
in love with death

under western skies

she cried novellas
in Kiswahili
telling stories
of her grandfather
who lost his mind
one rainy day walking
on the floor
of the Atlantic
looking for
the rest of himself
she lost her mind
climbing stairs to a star
saying god
had promised her
an interview
and this was going to be
her big break

so she broke down
when he didn't
show up
now she wears
straight-jackets
to church on Sundays
my grandmother
was a bowlegged
African woman
with gray hair
trembling
teaching her
grandchildren
how to survive
in this crazy
world.

Black angels with sky blue feathers

I met a black angel
with sky blue feathers
crying vodka tears
her bruised body
scarred with red
medu neters
I was licking
her software
she was performing
cataleptic cunnilingus
on my cerebral
cytococcus
causing seismic
sexual syrigmus
as computer generated
sphinxes followed
click tongue phoenixes
flying out of her womb

her thoughts
bled in circles
as scarlet scarabs
hid her heart in the ashes
of seven octillion orgies
with navy blue army ants
protecting mental ovaries

her onyx ovals
occulated octaves
of the original orgasm
that occupied her mind
she shrunk wrapped her soul
placed it on needle points

then slowly inserted it
into my eyeballs
to show me how
real her life was

her words
bum rushed my ears
my body evaporated
as her phlegmatic
stanzas ejaculated
purple shadows of self
written in barcode
and french
hieroglyphic echoes
she shook earthquakes
and tears
out of my mind
had me standing
in one spot
walking away
from myself
a thousand times
snorting
a thousand lines
of alliteration
deepening my abyss

her catharsis
healing my ochlesis
clamoring for sanity
as she orchestrated operas
of osteoplasty in origami
giving me ovarian cancer
she was a permed hair rasta
deep in concentration

I wanted to imprint her
with my genetic information
and pour libations
of my soul's continuation
on her soul's constellations
but her diction
kept messing with
my concentration

speaking of
mulatto mirrors
and albino shakespears
in beenies
saying things like
"wherefore art thou
my niggaz"
babbling in sanskrit
clock ticks
brainstorming
jigsaw puzzles
of antiquity

spitting blue-haired
haloed hermaphrodites
hemorrhaging
gothic hallelujahs
wearing xerox copies
of slave beatings
to hide her true feelings

singing the allegories of
misled Mexican women
in strawberry fields
playing in red clay
because sometimes

bloodlines are too
precious to paint with.

Her life

She opens eyes
and pushes back lids
gave sound movement
and rhythm her kids

she babysat gravity
and her cousin gravitation
turned the ignition
that started creation

she slow danced with oceans
sings songs with feelings
held the hands of time
while theorizing with rhyme

she broke bread with bread
set the universe free
when it was trapped
in a spider's web

she made love to reason
flirted with curses
talked sense into nonsense
cast spells on churches

she played chess with stars
slap boxed with god
sipped tea with suns
has universes trapped
within her lungs

she punched holes
in imagination

mirrored mirrors
hugged smell
caught daylight
as night time fell

she hangs out with atoms
at the bottom of existence
they call her dregs
she sews up black holes
time travels through eggs
they call her sperm

she burns and burns
like a comet
she used to chill with winds
now she snorts planets

she is addicted to death
dying from a disease
called life.

Woman hold her head and cry

Her lurid bony finger
grasped his warm flesh
her damned eyes
stared into the void
of his empty soul
her essence shot to death
she wept
her salty tears
and his lips caress
for a moment
they gape open
a last breath of resurrection
no

the words are unsaid
she cries
then waits an eternity
frozen in a cold sweat
as her soul follows his
half way to purgatory
then a memory
once she held
and tenderly kissed
the darkened body
of this blood covered baby
prematurely born they said
now she tries tirelessly
to jerk life into this
the prematurely dead.

Secret of life

I want to find
the secret of life
and give it to you
want to stand
in the twilight
and dance with
your silhouette
to mellow jazz tunes
As Billie hums
to the moon

I want to inhale
your thoughts
and do ménage a trois
with the beat
of your heart

do you know
that I am drunken
by your sweet
wet whisper
that makes
my kernels flicker
and dance like that
thick tangerine smoke
that dives off the tip
of an incense stick

you are like syrup
on my lips
petals on my sheets
and that fragrance
that makes my heart skip
when I am with you
I forget I am a man

and view myself
as the sand
in your hour glass

just hoping
hoping your love
does not run out

I want to walk slowly
through your
primordial waters
and taste
the sweet honey suckle
that's between your knees
catch your passionate
life energies
in my palms
as they pulsate
into blues and greens

I want to read you psalms
and Songs Of Solomon
take you to secret places
in distant lands
where the sunset is purple
the earth is roan
the rivers moan
as they plunge
deep into the sea

I want to be that leaf
that dies inside
your fountain of life
kiss your succulent lips
your hands
your eyelids
and rub your soul
into a paste
that will put you

to sleep for weeks

I want to float
on your smoke
sail on your horizons
and dip
thin beams of light
into your existential circles

you make me want to
cheat myself
lie to myself
ask why to myself
you make me not want
to be myself
but be the self
that you want me to be

and your smile
your smile is like silk
on my fingertips
gives me that
warm feeling inside
that feeling of
I believe I can fly
walk upside down
in the sky
touch the clouds
with my tongue
and sing songs
that would make
angels want to cry

but alas
it is impossible
for me to approach you
for I could not withstand
your smile
your blush

or the energies
you exude

so I will be content
with the pleasure of being
the thought
the life behind these eyes
that are so awed
by your existence.

Cataclysm

You make me see cataclysms
and surrealisms with
my eyes closed tight
witness armageddon
the fires of hell
and ten thousand
heavens last night
I was dazed
and half-crazed
in this place where
sweet nectars drip
honey streams flow
and chocolate fingers slip
in and out of the mouth
of nature's forbidden south

my flesh your nails tore
and I swore
I saw you levitate
your orifice an opiate
that makes me
want to overstate
how my mentals elevated
my soul was consecrated
and ascended to a place
where few get to taste
the fumes of faith
watch silver sunsets
and sip the effervesce
of a black bird's nest

men have found heaven
between those hips
those full juicy lips
that make moons eclipse
in threes like ellipse

vice lose their grips
angels be pouting
mortal men shouting
Christ walked on water
but I swam in your fountain
climbed your holy mountain
and if I come too soon
it's because I'm consumed
in the fruit of my doom
that which will bring me death
the thing I can forget
that makes me question
things be

is this a fix
does god exist
is he a man or just a myth
or is he really a she
who is really you

cause girl... that stew
will send a man to Bellevue
you give me mind sicknesses
I need nine witnesses
to all types of mental spasms
if you were a computer chip
I'd be a cybergasm
if you were a beam of light
I'd spread you like a prism
if you were a sound wave
my decibels would
ride your rhythm

I would give 23
of my chromosomes
to be home alone
with even your clone

your groove is like static

electromagnetic propulsion
travels at the speed of light
and gives me regal convulsions
and sensations
there has to be an explanation
and if so I want to know
are you an angel or a UFO
because you've got that
out of this world loving
that has this brotha bugging
I want to be the dough
that swells inside your oven

your glue is like a spell
cast from a witches coven
and that thick black sap
that's trapped
beneath your skirt
oh how much is it worth
because it is
the cure for cancer
oh it is the answer
to all of my woes
I would forgive all my foes
and walk without clothes
simply to sniff it with my nose

you make me see
circular squares
and five sided triangles
statues that walk
and star shaped
rectangles
birds that bark
and trees that float
strips of DNA
and even Japanese popes

I've even seen a mummy

in a bee colony
searching for your loving
and he told me it was honey
and as strange as it may sound
the brother was on the money.

Melody

Your essence still lingers
inside my soul's pagoda
an orchestra of
sentimental obeah
you wounded me
and this, my eulogy

some say
I ought not to love thee
for, they can't see why
I am trapped by the beat
of your drum
mesmerized by
the magnesium in your cum
been practicing yoga
trying to get over
this feeling
this diatribe
my disposition
in this position

with quaint memories
bathing my brain
hiding my hurt
behind stoic smiles
of encrypted pains

for once you were a mountain
of maroon earth in the palm
of my hand
which I honey massaged
into a pulp
and rubbed all over my face
absorbed you
through osmosis
opening new dimensions to

orgasmic psychosis
easing tensions
of mental erections
with diatonic tones

for you were music
and you moved me
and when my days were dull
one glimpse of you my love
was like heroin in my skull
I would give you
my sight
my sound
my being
and spend
the rest of existence
on a life machine
I have lost you
and in that
I have lost myself.

If I

If I made love to you
it would be like me
sticking my tongue into your soul
knelt in prayer
inside the flame of a candle
my spirit
chasing your essence
in infinite ciphers
until eternity was cross-eyed

if I made love to you
it would be like
me injecting steam
into your veins
you resisting the pains
by tightening your eyes
clenching your teeth
sinking your nails deep
into the tender cheeks
of a pitted peach
and licking the sweet nectars
that seep between
your ring and pinky finger
it would be 90 degrees
in the dead of winter

if I made love to you
it would be like
spending the rest of your life
inside of a cube of ice
while complaining
about the heat
more like
looking into the eyes of god
taking off your skin
walking in wind

with your eyes open
sipping a tall glass
of adrenaline
as you feel the sweet sting
of my saccharin
inside your hemoglobin

if I made love to you
the earth would turn to blue
your soul would split in two
and seep through
the corners of my mind
into the bottles of my spirituality

I want to love you
so that you can soak in
the waters of my thoughts
and swim in the music of my
feelings.

Black woman

The woman who stands on air
and proclaims she is from the sun
the woman that has no fears
and forces the Nile river to run
backwards

at the sound of her voice
leaves rejoice
at her bucolic grandiose

with legs as tall as
Lebanese cedar
and a soul so deep
would make god
want to read her
like his Bible
and be her first disciple

she swings those African hips
and turns rain into frost
Christ climbed off the cross
and depicted her the boss
the savior divine
though he turned water into wine
she had done much more
but her story is untold

she purified the soul
turned tears into gold
blood into rum
and played a saxophone
like a drum
made pyramids levitate
from the chakras
that she hummed

she sang the blues
that made prison walls bleed
many have tried
but did not succeed

and still ask why
mountains crumble into dust
as her sad lullabies
resound throughout the earth
she gave birth
to music itself

she is so passionate and complex
that if you are down and vexed
she can smile, and it's like sex

her thoughts are so cryptic
and outside of the norm
that she had to write them down
in cuneiform
and medu neter
is a black man's
love letter to her
for millenniums
before antiquity
she has been the epitome
of mankind
the esoteric paradigm
the supreme
black woman.

Her pain

It slowly creeps toward her
whispering horror stories
to her subconscious soul
time stepped outside of itself
to bear witness to the terror
of her agony
her pain

which was played in slow motion
over old muddy blue tunes
those murmurs of
undecipherable shrieks
intonations of nothingness
that gnaw at your being
inside half lit drunken stairwells

she heard bells
as the whip claimed refuge
deep in the flesh
of her tender leathery back
opening old wounds
and establishing new colonies
in this grotesque topography
that now oozed
the stains of Africa's hurt

and like sharpened fish hooks
its tips hurriedly grabbed
rugged splinters of her flesh
and splattered them all over
the macabre cobweb
infested ceiling

daubed naked walls
absorb the aftertaste
of her raw spirited blood

blood that had a thousand eyes
blood that cried out
in its own silent upheaval
blood that had grown
used to this serum
trembling and fearful
lost in a dream
that seemed endless

her withered toes
were kept warm
by a steam that rose
from a pool of
newly battered blood
vibrant and bulging with life

she did not cry
her body did
every muscle twist and turn
resisting the venomous sting
she seemingly collapsed
inside of her insides
her eyes bleared
as her toes
whispered eulogies
to the damp earth
only inches away

she swung from
a rusted meat hook
arms popped
from their sockets
in this, the shed
of her torture
every vein in her
protested
as her wrist pled
under the fatigue

of the parched rope
that devoured her flesh
a warm crimson liquid
cascaded down
the back of her
cement calves
making its way between
her ankle bone
and her hardened heel
then slowly trickled down
her robust feet

she fought back her tears
and seconds were like years
she heard streams
and streams of screams
only if she could grow wings
and fly away from her pain

then the whip came
planting itself deep
inside a previous lash
stinging feverishly
water squirted
from her padlocked eyes

her back arched in
mouth pried open with anguish
lines of dried saliva
maroon lips gray from thirst
she hollers in silence
in a sound so pure
only the dead
could comprehend.

It was raining food stamps...

It was raining
food stamps last night
but brothers
were too busy rescuing
black leaders
from prostate cancer
cancer?
that's a sign of the times
but we only know gang signs
that's why they got us
crippled blood
so I figured
I've got to start practicing
voodoo and santeria
acupuncture and meditation
levitation and time travel
chant mantras
tap into my past lives... and
dust off my
how to catch
a bullet manual
because the NYPD
got quotas now
now... they have
Klan rallies in precincts
while priests are sent
to rally my clan
damned by this
dysfunctional diatribe
nobody seems to see
that my tribe is dying
more and more brothers
are drawing closer and closer
to extinction
painting pictures

of a futureless future

to pass the time
everybody is trying
to find god
but god
got his own problems
he's trying to find a way
to downsize heaven
more like
no affirmative action
for self-righteous
mothaf#@kas
he got angels
working temp
because full time angels
need benefits
judgement day
might be canceled
because...
the artist formerly known as Prince
does not want to do the half time show
plus he go that Y2K problem
the devil is on strike
demanding better working
conditions
so we need to get a plan
because everything is going crazy
even the trees speak ill of the wind
the birds no longer fly south
they are refuting
the concept of direction
refusing to sing
saying something in the water
told them they were free
so now they write rhymes
inking feathers so blue
they call us black birds

who used to hang
with Jim Crow
faxing our feelings
that beat through drums
like hearts do.

Slam-o-nomics 495

I can only be understood
by albino transvestites
who think in melanin intervals
by sistas who wear head wraps
around their wombs
and nose rings in their eyelids
to smell
what the future looks like

I take bubble baths
in decaffeinated estrogen
to keep in touch
with my feminine side
there is a revolution
going on inside my womb
I think I am suffering from
multiple slam disorder

I slam schizophrenic dinosaurs
in time tunnels
and bowlegged elephants
who study butterflies for a living
giving deaf poets
sound strokes and cataracts
in their mind's eye
I battle African wordsmiths
in places like Lilongwe
and Madagascar
in villages where it rains fire
for six months out of every year
where the people are so futuristic
that no two poets
speak the same language
so we had to slam in sound

I've been to places where

we slammed in silence
shhhhhhhhhhhhhhhhhh!
because fake poets
get disqualified
for not thinking
loud enough
they say concrete
breeds amnesia
so I have two
questions for you
do you remember
when the US flag
was red, black
and green? no!
do you remember
when the Bible
was a pamphlet? no!
then you can't say
shit to me then
because you have
forgotten who you are
I used to babysit god
back in the days
when the pope was Muslim
and time was slow-motion

now...
I recycle time
and sell it in capsules
like abortions
in snowflakes
my poetry is traded
on stock markets
in three different galaxies
seas filled with African bones
chalking word-o-glyphics
on the walls of human souls
mosquitoes used to smuggle
my poetry into Cuba

like nuclear arms
arm wrestling scorpions
for their stings
I feel like I'm being chased
by a swarm
of third eyes
sewn shut
trying to see
what I'm saying
see what I'm saying?
I tattoo needles
under my tongue
to spit poems
that stick to your
subconscious
I start forest fires
in the subways
and throw open mics
in volcanoes
because...

It's been raining
weak poets for too long now

so a new generation
of poets have come up
wearing dashikis
and army fatigues
rocking afros
and kilts
on Nostrand avenue
selling incense
and performing
open heart surgery
on the sidewalk
I am that voodoo priestess
who had to raise
herself from the dead *twice*

after having
clandestine meetings
with the NYPD
blue is how I'm feeling
selling sea moss
laced with
middle passage stories

trying to free
those poets who shackle
their talents
in rooms filled
with cordless candles
burning suicide notes
to dead end jobs
I just made
my first down payment
on my second pyramid

and I know you didn't get that!

because this is written
in binary codes
in computer languages
computers don't speak
my language is metaphor
poets be on all fours
with razor blades
under their tongues
trying to cut my throat
but I'm the dominatrix
in this matrix
I give poets electrically
transmitted diseases
like Y2K
meaning you too
kindergarten kid
so call me the millennium bug
but my phone calls me

at least twice each day
asking me questions like
what is tomorrow's middle name?

and I know you didn't get that

because...
I can only be understood
by albino transvestites
who think in melanin intervals
by sistas who wear head wraps
around their wombs
and nose rings in their eyelids
to smell
what the future looks like.

Notes on my piano

Amidst the shadows i danced with death
making a mockery of mine own lethargy
wondering
what if death were man's only escape
from this wretched life?
fettered by my shortcomings
i live a baffled existence
grappling with the yeahs
and the nays of mortals
is it not man who makes the moment?
or is it the moment
that makes man?
what if death does not exist?
what then?
my understanding sits
down the barrel of a loaded gun
laying wait
as i stand here
rearranging my thoughts
to match my insipid existence
i live because life is all i know
and i know there has to be more to life
than this.

Book IX

THE WOMAN WHO ISN'T WAS

(1999-2000)

Uneven dreams

I stood
in the scorpion of her
lost in the memories of her inertia
deep in the wet of her soft
flesh flushed against mine
eyes filled with emotions
tears intact
I'm sorry
I can't love you
still moving deep into the tender
of this swan's purple
fingers whispering
teething the flesh
from my back
like cautious candles
looking for excuses
she, the medicine
woman with juniper hands
and at the moment of orgasm
she promised me that
when she died she would
will her womb to give birth
to me in the next life
so she could love me unconditionally
and that was 17,000 years ago
when we existed as echoes
in a windstorm
on an exploding planet
two universes over
embracing the thread of her is
I danced with illusions

embroidered in mystery
murdered by many men
she too was alone
searching
unaware
walking into walls
with a broken heart in a steel cage
this daughter of a blacksmith
laying atop my easel
like a parable
interwoven into
the paper of my being
bleeding
I read her two chapters
from a book of zebras
she stopped me
said she spent
the past 400 years
giving out eyes
at the gate of a city
which strangely
explained the first
three years of my life
caught my breath
drowning
woke up in a coffin
cotton stuffed in my nostrils
eyes removed
insides empty
she was gone
and the silence
tasted like embalming fluid
on my lips
a tender knocking

400

like a kiss, at the door
of my conscience
it was an old woman
wrinkled and waxy
red shawl
white-haired
beaming, transfixed
I was
buddha
she handed me a liquid marble
that emitted so much light
that I broke out in tears
crying for no reason
crying because I understood
crying because I didn't understand
cried so hard it became 1920
she, a jazz singer under red lights
dancing with strands of cigar smoke
winked
it became 1828
she now my wet nurse
smiling... I screaming
brought forward
broke her heart at the prom
brought back
broke her heart
before I met her
just so she would
keep her distance
died twice as a child
avoiding her
she aborted me once
moved to China
changed her race

just so our paths wouldn't cross
just so our crosses wouldn't path
until one London evening

I got a card in the post
pictured: a slim Asian woman
with stolen eyes
red robe
eyes stolen
from a lover, me
drawing circles
on the foreheads
of the dust quilted children
knitted from ether
blowing around in circles
at the gate of the city
three thousand years earlier
and in her left shoulder
burning bright blue
a black candle
waxed with tears
forever frozen black
she pulled me
into the photo
the photo fell
falling
into a small slice
of another universe
she was burning
embers floating like bubbles
above her head
pulling pins from her aura
each pin a lifetime wasted
each lifetime in the form of a song

each song an ember
each ember blazed singing
emitting so much light
I blinked
and in that instant
seventeen faces
of this same woman
eons ago
centuries ago
years ago
futures ago
and before I could say
what is your name
she vanished

and
I'm in a diner
she is serving black coffee
and donuts
to a trucker with a
white beard
and a red cap
tagged
made in China
she walked over
to my table
and gently placed
a plate with two eggs
bleeding like eyes
looking up at me
I looked up at her
have I seen you
some place before?
she said no and

walked out of the diner
like a jazz singer
like a wet nurse
like a coroner
like the daughter
of a blacksmith
she left me
with my heart
chained
to her pillow
I'm sorry
I can't love you
maybe in another lifetime.

Gardens

Trees that bloom whispers
pages and pages of light bulbs
what if the wind was
more than one person?
telephone birds
ringing as they fly
contrived insects
wrestling echoes
on a theoretical floor
sound glued to time
with eyes like those
she could salvage infinity
and the elevator
would not have moved
most men
want to have orgasms
I want her to teach me
how to evaporate
how to make love
to her molecules
like three angels
in a glass of triangular wine
close my eyes
and walk
through this wall
but there are
too many fingers
in my soul
to explain
what it means
when she says

I understand.

The scarring ritual

She is magic music
standing like jupiter
shifting her soul
from side to side
like a tie-dyed angel
hiding infinity inside her her
carving spirits in the wind
been recruiting the sand
watched god go blind
wooden verandas
stitched in her perfume
and when she stepped
out of that jar of electronic oil
and showed me
the fullness of her breast
took my hands
and slowly slipped them over
the soft frolicking curves
of her hips
sent shock waves
and vibrations
splitting through
the corridors of me
like circular sound
erupting into silence
and she was there
speaking in whispers
speaking in meaning
speaking in soundless sounds
said, *every time a woman ovulates*
a universe is created

closed her eyes
and when she opened them
I saw god for the first time

and then she left
and the stories came
in flashes of light
stories she never told
stories of a scarring ritual
stories of a drumming ceremony
stories of mud-paint
stories of a childhood
I lived
in a distant life
a life I felt like
she lived for me
so now I live for her
hoping one day I'll see her
in the sunset
in the wind
in a cough
a smile
a wink
in anything
and I can't really sleep
until I've seen her.

Forever flowers

Atom bomb
in the belly
of the blue baby
dripping sepia
mixed with surrender
naked clocks
and forever flowers
facing marbled men
the great suggestion
is made of legs
made of rubles
have you seen
the way these people move
walking, talking
chalk falling from their
cage powder lips
into yellowed palms
silent skin
braided tight
melting, they move
like blurs, they blur
eyes spinning
like steam
raping the radiator
the only language
they know is heat
and it's a cold world
rolling around slowly
in the hands
of an invisible childhood
when we all lived

in the ruins of clouds
and the words of the windmill
were characteristically
feminine
like circles
designed by
the ghost-like boy
and his coin-sister
their mom
with two eyes in each palm
an extra leg
she's mostly fingers
weaving memories
naming the tracks in her arms
she's been soul searching
looking for forever
found it in her children
realized that they were her
forever flowers
they grow
in the most
mysterious places.

Disappearing woman

Stitch sista
ink woman in this
inverted world
scrambling her thoughts
summaries of a previous future
time ticking in her toenails
changing like
different size circles
drawn on her pelvis
ovaries are creation chambers
so god has to be a woman
and she ain't crazy
she just been
dodging anthills
avoiding the anteater
watched cardinals
fly away with strands of her self
returned as popes
wearing white frocks
and candle suits

she lies inches
away from a burning church
reading the wind
with her eyes closed
cause she's still got that
magic in her blood
voodoo in her bones
hands vanishing
back and forth
like an orchestra of insects

patching holes
in her force field
forced into fields
to push plows
so now she paints
the wind clay

clock woman
carrying maps
of the universe
beaten into her flesh
with directions to their souls
hidden in her spinal column
she said they ain't got no souls
so now she walks around backwards
with two glasses of god
two tobacco leaves
a leafless Bible
a green gourd
filled with her self
saw-dust and see-water

using this old cotton branch
to beat off this mindless flock
of albino vultures
covered with mechanical sores
covered with soot and talc
moving in a slow
screeching meander
blood in their tail feathers
every step cursed
smelling like murder
looking like death
this appearing woman

412

standing on tilt
like a haunted house in heels
wearing a red vintage dress
racing toward me
like an evaporating bull

then... like magic
she becomes
a thousand tiny
blue butterflies
then back to woman
then
a floating field
of flying crystal splinters
then back to woman
then
a dancing circle
of twisted lights
then back to woman
then
she becomes
me, I mean us

we have figured out
other ways
of communicating
with the dead
been talking to the dust
tapping into the trees
kinda like strumming
god in reverse
on the umbilical
of this unborn baby
born

with his arms in his mouth
on the inside of his outsides
in the arms of this wind woman
watching these boys
standing on ladders
denying themselves manhood

you'll never be a man
until you learn
to respect your mother.

Mother

Growing up
without a mother
is like going to
public school
naked.

Emotional alchemy

Like perfumed cannibalism
the monthly triangular Christ
hovers over geometric
dream shapes
dressed in tunics
versions of a symbolic self
bleeding baskets of prayers
dead men under her knees
like drawings of martians
growing coffins
in crystal cities
surrounded by
vanishing fields
he wears a glass mask
dancing with
bald-headed women
painting them purple
covering them with feathers
they remind him of her
like unfinished softness
drowning in orange paper
paper paper
kisses her
three times
to forget her name
there is a difference between
making love and making love
wanted to love you
but he had to volunteer
poured out cupid
on strange women

using up their primary colors
drew them in pencil
because he wanted
to love you
but you wanted
to love
who he was
not who he is.

Angels in blur

I met her in the mouth of a hug
in the backyard of a clock
the clasped hands of a
Chinese Friday
at the end of an
invisible phone call
this solar system of a woman
said she found the cure for sight
blinded by her words
a hovering tongue
she was born mute
moonlit womb
guiding the fetus
stomach expanding
walking on cobwebs
there is language
in the tick of her
carrying elbows
ticking

expanding
like the minds of children
unable to move
she's morphing
changing
into life-jackets
into streams
into spider-elephants
butterfly-bulls
scorpion-fish
rice-angels

kimono-camels
into forever
with windows
to the breast milk
of her soul
she had olive eyes

will see things
you'll never
be able to see.

The woman who isn't was

Filled my flashlight with ink
wrote a whale
do the dolphins
have to understand the ocean
to keep the beat?

in the key of collodion glass
my soul sits
seasoned with magnetic snail paint
vibrating skeletons
the color of time
her tears cried her
in vibrato

like a silent Bible
broken
she ate herself whole
arms first
legs last
like little
laboratory mice
in glass suits
wearing green houses
what a spectacle
she's too blind
to see that raindrops
are shaped like infinity signs

she sighs
breathes out a train
inhales the city
three times ink
we traded orgasms
like invisible pigeons
passing around
a push button Jesus

wake up
god is only a cough-drop
what if the universe
is only half the question
and the other half the womb

like she-quation dentistry
she slowly removed my brain
showed it to the centipede
a legless blindfolded chair
with bicycle blood

I'd recite my fingerprints
in reverse gravity
to be within a thousand years
of what she sounds like

me
a black duck
with one wooden leg
standing in the snow
I pretended I couldn't kiss
so she wouldn't fall in love
or so she wouldn't fall in promise

because of what?
no... because of... of
isn't that then maybe because of shouldn't
or is it then maybe because shouldn't isn't isn't
or maybe it is?
probably isn't isn't isn't
I'm not sure
but shouldn't shouldn't be what isn't isn't
because of of
of course not

it's not how deep the ocean is
it's how the stones

at the bottom
feel about themselves

touch me
we did not disappear
we merely figured out how
to grow our cities upside down
in the sand

so now I wake up mornings
talking to the curtains
talking to the candles
trying to take
the water out of
the ice cubes

trying to think myself
into being her
but I can't
because if I did
she would be
missing me then

the woman who isn't was.

Little white girls *(for colonial Europe)*

They stood in the courtyard
in groups of six
slowly powdering their
thin pale faces
with the ashes
of lynched men
gulping down
large glasses
of the finest red wine
staining their uneven
off-white teeth
strolling around
on colonial stilts
refilling their glasses
with blue decadence
giggling blood
dripping down their lips
chapped
with their odd shaped heads
in frocks too wide for their vision
the taste of vomit
in their nostrils
cheeks beaten red
questioning eyes
forcibly kept calm
stoic
doing the shut-eye shuffle
they keep losing sight
of what's real
and what's really real
they hate the smell of Europe
so they erect tall buildings
these little white girls
who purchase smiles
and take baths in tubs
filled with the blood of Africans

hiding our history
on the envious walls
of their cathedrals
little white girls
who have eaten
human flesh
yet they have never
tasted freedom.

Metal medusa

Black woman
riding a mindless moon
memorized every moment
passed them down to her babies
because somebody's
been painting the trees white
the fumes will kill you

nigga-deem-us
hanging from a
sick-amor tree
with more Moors
than any one tree
could bear
keep in mind
that machines
have no morals

so you can't blame
the cotton jinn
she lies, knees spread
stretch marks all over her sorcery
black magic babies
born to die
born to be strangled
by the roots of trees
drawn in the palms
of their mothers hands
haunted by
her voodoo children
she stands staring
at the sun, her soul
like weeping strips of metal
blown by an invisible wind
blood in her mouth
blood in her nostrils

blood on her teeth
blood in her eyes
in her throat
choking
coughing up her eyeballs
spitting out the sun
spitting out Bibles
spitting out babies
spitting out her skeleton

fingers broken
fingernails broken off
in her thighs
crawbing, ripping, tearing
into the fiber of her
not so dancing
this cruel dance
no more
can't dance
no more

still holding her dead babies
hugging them so tight
she could feel them in her shins
six shotgun barrels
to the side of her head
knee deep in colonialism
she hums a song so profound
her hair changes
from grey to blue
to blood red

if I had the wings of a dove
I would fly, fly away
pulling the auction block
out of her hair
the cotton gin
out of her soul
the chicken wire

out of her flesh
click

she tightens her eyes
clenches her fists
bites into her bottom lip
braces her soul
I'll resist you forever

BLAAW!

white silence
only her fists remain
kicking
screaming
I would fly, fly away
I'm free... at last.

'Twas a morning blue
in the morning dew
when I danced a folly
frolic mine
my mind behest
her soul undressed
she said those words
a thousand times
as they played a song
so sweet so soft
an evil thought
that split my tongue
through trees so dark
and waters cold
a continent through
rivers run
then in her eyes
the naked truth

'twas a moment
dull and bold
then I realized
that she was I
the woman I loved
about to be sold.

Auction block

Insanity on a stick

Strings of light women
cinder bubble children
heat steam men
melting into water spirits
walking limb-less
into this tumble shaped world
filled with
electronic sand seekers

fire fluid bird people
shifting flesh webs
shifting see-through bodies
filled with
liquid light particles
like floating sound
in semi-solid form

forming these
tiny microscopic
kerosene sliders, sliding
some walk on slant
some on vertical
others on side wind
on the up
on different wavelengths
on multiple plains
in multidimensional patterns
in all possible possibles

they came changing
with wings, horns, furs,
fishtails, tentacles, paws,
fists, fangs, feathers
in colors the mind can't conceive

like the color *plev*

beyond symbol
or perception
but for some reason
in that moment
I saw them all
en regalia

in their deep purple splendor
in slippery silks
moving maroons
strolling slowly down
this twisted platform
like an exodus
towards the real

then a whisper
there are no empty spaces
in the universe
it's just that
we were all
born blind
welcome.

Coffin

Once, I locked myself
in a vacuum
with a gun
committed suicide
and the strangest
thing happened
I came back
to life.

What ?

In the haze of a half sleep
I stumbled upon my soul
dressed in dogma
hair braided in blood
humming shackles
she had the underground railroad
hidden in the roof of her mouth
It's all an illusion, she said,
pay close attention to the number six

I said, *what ?*

she said,
e backwards is the sum of you
to the hieroglyphics
divided by three times tomorrow
plus now expanded by the root
of a black bird
on a chain gang
bench-pressing 3/5 of forever
behind bars

I said, *what ?*

she said, *life sentences and death sentences*
are merely paraphrases of the same thing
genocide, topped with esoterica
is genocide just the same
it matters not how beautifully

worded it is worded
their words can't hide their intentions
these belligerent bastards
been teaching genetics
since kindergarten classes

432

I said, *what ?*

she said,
you remember ?
yes you do Brad

ba ba black sheep
have you any wool
yes sir, yes sir
three bags full
father, son, and holy ghost

because all of a sudden
Mary, has a little lamb
whose wool was white as snow

that my friend
was the first cloning experiment
they've been copying us for the longest
trying to steal us

but no matter how they
manipulate time and space
they can't touch me
my existence is etched
in ecto-chrome
in between visibility and blindness
close your eyes and I'm still there
blackness is everywhere

in the visible
and in the invisible
so don't worry
they can't kill me
this is already my afterlife.

I said, *what ?*

Devil's workshop

This is the devil's workshop
Salvador Dali and Picasso
devised a scheme
painted Socrates white
which means that Shakespeare
is really Bill Gates
but he's hard to detect
because now he's
micro soft, word

don't trust them
they've been
faking reincarnation
for thirty thousand dollars
you can practice being god
at Harvard's divinity school

many ways of
manipulating the now
they come amongst us to de-clone
open your eyes, me
none of this is real

slavery never happened
this is all a drill
that we're putting them through
to see if they've got souls
spirit over flesh friend
don't trust them
they've been
abducting martians
using their genetics
to control the weather
whether you believe it or not
it's up to you

they've been
using sonograms
microwaves
and cell phones
to reconfigure
your psychological
make up

kinda like
magnetic oppression
through electrical pork
and you are
worried about them
cloning sheep, funny

they've been
cloning the eggs
and you've been
eating the clones
why do you think
the tomatoes know
how to breathe
under water?

Spirit fiction

They changed his brain
turned his arms into sickles
into needles
into never-horses dancing
with angels in his teeth
melting like babies
on an olive branch

holding their noses
like vampire spiders
spinning webs of glass
brush-mark mantis
black ants crawling
on the naked torso
of these see-through women
inside inkwells
in the roots of trees
jumping out of bottles

this is the dance
this is where worlds merge
this is where we cross breed
this is normal man
in dream sleep
in sleep sleep

like cherubim
and centaurs
wrestling goldfish
fact is
on dark days
even dark umbrellas
transform into
puffy white cushions
into moons trapped
in blocks of ice

even lines are illusions
paint them red
and change every single
sky-walking elephant
in this motha-stop

if your back is to the world
how can you sleep?
I mean sleep sleep
this isn't reality
it's only a suggestion

propped up
on blue fascinations
like the supernatural ablaze
outstretched and vivid
like breath monsters
floating over strip houses
or rock men
splitting into numerals

crucifixions stay constant
like seed symbolism
they kill us in the streets
because it is easy
death used to be the theme
now it's the cure
for morphing men
with bugs on the skull
obsessed with
the shape of shoes
obsessed with
the color of skin
eat my memories
fuel your addictions
enhance your fears
rip my head off
shove your ice cold sword

down my carcass
tear my soul out
by its strings
but you can't
change who I am.

Lights out

27 floating children
parading with dirty hair
magic uniform skin
palms painted yellow
braille-matrix
African scar codes
written all over their bodies
channeling spirits
dressed in tattered rags
sewn together
with the bones of old slaves
who sat in circles
in the middle of graveyards
in the backroom of the galaxy
piecing themselves together
under the blue flame
of an ancient kerosene lamp

lights out!

we mumbled in the forest
until the trees started speaking
until the earth came alive
came back through scorpion stings
surviving against all odds
because we've got to survive
we have to survive
we must survive
cause while
Christ was crouched
in a corner of
a cold cathedral
next door to the Kremlin
riding a wooden bike
with a cross nailed
to his back

cranking out
the music
that keeps
the birds in this
end us tree, singing
we were trying
to save the world
because that's what
true freedom is about
isn't it?

lights out!

who dreamt up
this place
who is messing
with the future
with these
oxygen-making machines
melting women
vertical oceans
human zoos
dogs that don't bark
trees with leaves only
no limbs
no roots

we can now
compete with the sun
light is light
that's what they say
but these are
the same bastards
who be putting
the devil in
the baby formula
in their white suits
and parchment
paper hair

440

trying to control
that which they
can't control
ripping off
my bandages
telling me that
in the future
I'll be in a jar
labeled, DNA

so I had to flip it
on them like
AND

the mind is intangible
they said, *how ?*

I said
*how how became how
could be how became became became
because how became became became
could be how because became because
because because became because
how how became how
but that doens't
necessarily mean
that all three
are related
in the way we think
of relationships
get it?!*

*SHIPS
that's how we got here
not necessarily over water
but over ether
how many solar systems
can you fit in one galaxy
let alone a whole universe*

lights out!

and that's when
the transparent man
slid under the door
like a mystic on acid
freeloading off divinity
with his invisible umbrella
and his pockets filled
with styrofoam gods
chi-ching

read them like runes
no crown atop his head
wore them on his teeth
17 brains
3 hearts
and his newspaper print skin
like a nazi propaganda machine
who's running the show?
does it matter?
yes it does!

well, let me put it
for you this way sonny
shape shifting
is only a matter
of matter
manipulation
through sound
we hummed ourselves
in and out of existence

we be smoke people
sorcerers
magicians
witchdoctors
druids

442

poets
levitats
luminaries
griots
your grandfather
was one of us
we do the
purple rain dance
passing
peace pipes
like blunts
on city blocks
puff-puff
pass
puff-puff
present
puff-puff
future

we live lifetimes
between each breath
realized that
melanocytes are really
microscopic black holes
so we can be
in every part
of the universe
at the same time
who decided
this was earth anyway?

lights out!

Drug wars

Half of Tibet
India by the ankles
China in a head lock
Colombian strangle hold
heaven in a nickel bag
George Bush on the logo
left arm of god slung
in a black boot
bones, brothas, bullets
heroin
human paint
in human jars
filled with spirits
blue, yellow, indigo, reds
bending, bending clocks
propaganda books
old metal
typewriters
frozen

silent streets
levitating cars
slipping away
wind-walkers wrapped
in orange duct tape
white paint footsteps
invisible floors
forever standing like

Hong Kong
Kingston
Freetown
Brooklyn
London
Shanghai
smallpox turns

444

to crack cocaine
zombies in
purple plaster
in silent villages
lined with poppy fields
stuffed and crowded
with opal women

eyes taped shut
stapled to the land
their kids mutated like
wombs handcuffed
to the economy

soul prostitution
CIA
World Bank
Vatican
White House
Pentagon
United Nations

chances are
to them
we are all invisible
but most people
couldn't see that.

Trees

Two hundred thousand years ago
humanity was so evolved
that we started turning into trees
and contrary to popular belief
the trees run this planet
it's a secret society
and they are using
paper money
to keep us
spiritually at bay.

America

Shadows of horses
in mirage
superimposed over
slave ships
the concrete pope
in a coffin of mirrors
like brain surgery on a coin
like asking elephants
the meaning of currency
Spain was involved
England was involved
Europe's been eating ivory boats
for years
and the shadows complain
because history
should not be served
with ice cubes
on tea napkins
with caviar
mothers raped
by the ocean
so sons wear
ankle bracelets
to jog their
memories
how can
they forget
when these
same clouds
walk around
in the forest
pretending
the trees don't exist.

Black magician

The spirits came
in the form of
this old man
talking in spirals
transforming wind
into pictures
disintegrating
like blue delirium
or methodic madness
silver black eyes perched
on his cold charcoal face
like fallen angels
with their wings removed
this old man
half man, half ghost
half man, half glass
half man, half god
golden scorpions
trapped behind his metal eyes
like burn dance
balancing this strange
wooden-like instrument on his head
a pendulum
with no strings
no balls
but you could still hear the
click, click, click, click
clicking sound
his fire paint hair moving
back and forth
with every click
opened his mouth
and there lay three caterpillars
slowly becoming men
arms like power cables
paintbrush fingers dangling

like test tubes filled with fright
his thoughts
causing a halo
of perpetual sparks
to hover around his head
every spark
becoming a rosary bead
liquefies into water pellets
falling at the speed of existence
toward the granite floor
shattering into
slow-motion ice
then does the whole thing
in reverse
un-shattering
back to ice
back to water
back to rosary
back to spark
back to thought
back into his head
his two palms
became roses
one blue, one red, the other...
illusion
pulled a deck of cards
from the wind
closed his eyes
no tricks
watched his body
transform from
flesh
to fluid
to echo
and all that was left
was this deck of cards
all jokers.

Robot school

This is where they come
in droves
to get their souls tailored
to join this circus
to join the puppet machine
they die in silence
numb to their own humanity
socially engineered
genetically altered
like corn fields
like American dreams
like time
like fast food Christianity
chainsaw religion

ask the Vatican
babies born behind bars
pile them high
mountains of bodies
hollowed, burnt and black
nodding
while the United Nations
plays the remix of their pain
for the World Health Organization
this is genocide
ask the IMF

vampire is only a metaphor
for rich people
corporations need to sell shares
so now they are selling the slaves
to themselves
ask the World Bank
mothers like broken glass
in blood-filled gutters
shrouded in shawls

praying to a god who is being
lobbied by Phillip Morris
who is a member of the NRA
who is being paid off
by pharmaceuticals

and soon the apples
will taste like heroin
nicotine in the oranges
and they'll start growing
humans from trees
ask Lockheed Martin
and these aren't flies
these are cameras
ask the CIA
this is robot school
the tin factory
this is where they come
in droves
to get their souls tailored.

Mathestract

X7 4H
divided by cubed root
hello, jump
city city
where?
cardboard
explain
how?
odd numbers
hello hello
divided by jump
city city
invisible man walks by
a store window
sees himself
jump
is he there?
jump
trees
mechanics
glass-uncle
city city
explain explain
sound jump
numbers
square root squared
root root
plus or minus
explain
coins cats belts
hello hello
jump
fingers, blood
2mgs of liquid
death powder
cork metal

452

geese blue
water blue
moon
meter meter meter
hello jump
maps, old men, cigars
children
whose name is yellow?
excuse me?
are you still vanishing?
jump
maybe, maps
light-trees
gray
prime
explain
metal worms
clocks
forever silent guns
wait
what?
oh my friend
insanity is such a beautiful thing
is that you?
excuse me?
lunchbox lunchbox
city city
what
there is someone
jump
next life, next life
fingers
sound
hello
explain forever
what
explain holding
city city
jump

coin
heads tails heads tails heads tails
explain
close your eyes
stop
jump life
jump stop
jump death
jump stop
there is someone holding
explain
a gun
explain
to your
circles
columns
rows
head explain
square
octagon
triangles
circles circles
sound
stop
there is someone holding
explain
a gun
explain
to your head
explain
the person
explain
is you
explain
no!!!
stop
next life.

Mr. Computa

He got that crooked math
that sideways swivel stitch language
spells his name with all zeros
to trick himself
to throw off the ants
to eat away at time
he's always filing
trying to organize
the powder from his nails
into Bibles
broken stories
static hidden in his gums
a distorted tin of distance
clamped onto his teeth
look at that smile
this boneless man
bounded only by reason
for no particular reason
he'll never fully know
the mechanics of his life
or see the fiber of his being
practicing telepathy
through wires
you've got mail
Mr. Computa

with his cyber limp

his pixeled hum

always conspiring against himself

because he has no friends

he needs to wake up

and smell the gigabytes.

Book X

THE WOLF WHO CRIED BOY

(2001-2008)

The Negro unplugged

I am the negro unplugged
I am Toby and Tiger Woods
crucified to the speed of light
my telepathy is on the floor
of a methadone clinic
injecting the ace of spades, spaded
I am the knife in Caesar's back
the bullet through Kennedy's face
I am jheri curl juice
and hog-maws
Sambo with his eardrums stolen
I guess you can call me
the most deaf, fried chicken
dressed in nightmares and flames

I am the never not never
the always not not
I be who I say I is
because I am
a slave ship in the middle
of the Sistine Chapel
I am Stepin Fetchit
wearing blue prints
of the constitution
dying a death so beautiful
man we so beautiful
we suffer with our eyes closed
blindfolds, gold fronts
fronting because we have
to survive this constant Christ-ing

massacred martyrs us be
hence the thus, therefore, I am
Toussaint Louverture
fractured
hammered to the sky

french doors and all
1804 and all
I am Harriet, Condoleezza
rice fields, cane fields, cornrows
afros, the perm
the conk, the weave
and the pressing iron
irreligious and sacred, like
Garvey's bones on display
at the Louvre
I am Jimi Hendrix
guitar plugged into the ocean floor
galactic high hat, high hat
snare
kick drum
kick drum
snare
spirit
gentrified to Picasso

I am the double-headed
cubist in the belly
of ten shredded tomorrows
I am tomorrow yesterday
a burning church inside of
the whites only water fountain
a metal dream, a song so
bitter
we split the atom
the black
Baghdad
the Moorish now
Beirut on
a cotton gin
spliff between his teeth
facing his inquisitors

I am face paint and tribal scars
crack pipe and tribal scars

track marks and tribal scars
Harvard and tribal scars
I am Dubois
old, wrinkled
wearing the Black Star Liner
around his neck
to Lincoln's assassination
I am Malcolm at a Starbucks
in Harlem, the espresso machine
making love to his bullet wounds
I am a blind musician
with no song to sing
I am the black resistance
dreaming of white girls
with long flowing hair
like Rapunzel and Snow White
and Sleeping Beauty

Michael, wake up: the American
mind-fuck has rearranged your face
I am a bottle of bleaching cream
poured into the palms
of Jack Johnson
I am genocide
in every lyric that Big wrote
It's the ten crack commandments
I've been in this game for years
it made me an animal
there's rules to this shit
I wrote me a manual

I am the Rolling Stones
The Beatles, Bob Dylan
and Elvis Presley all in black face
I am the Black psyche
one-eyed, mouth of blood
whispering womb juice
into the fabric of Old Glory
I am a black boy

on a street corner
in Brooklyn
freestyling his way
back to god.

Black boy

He's a street corner, a stoop
a blindfolded blunt, a nuclear
bomb in the middle of Brooklyn
a thunderclap in the womb of death
A black boy, a tranquilized metaphor
the twice-ghettoed, shackled
to the midnight in his hands
shooting hoops, shooting off
at the mouth, middle passage
in his cornrows, maps back
to the interior, back to Shango
back to the spirits

multidimensional black boys
cotton seeds, tobacco sheds
apartheid, Jim Crow, church boy
field hands, crossover
like time travel in slave ship
tenements
he's a fifth of vodka
the black requiem lost
in fragments
of its own genius
he's government cheese and divinity
food stamps and infinity
immune to the cyanide
in the quarter water

the heat translates these dark boys
into small songs
into a canvas of spilled insanity
into the chaos trapped
in a star's heartbeat
all this chaos
this conjured oblivion
this resistance

amongst the dark boys
with their scrawny arms
sagging pants, scarlet
eyes squeezed tight
by cannabis
seeds of confusion
the perfume of wasted years
in his collar bone

and he's addicted
to street corners
and malt liquor
addicted to the taste
of his forefathers sweat
in the tobacco leaves
all that Hennessy, dreaming
beneath his tongue
next to the razor
next to the history of ancestors
planted below Wall Street
next to the memories of a father
he's never seen
and he wants
to go places
so he's writing his name
on everything that moves
penned his greatest verse
on the window of a train
watched it slide off
into the killing twilight
it said
dear world
what have I done
for you to hate me so?

he's a black buffalo
walking backwards
through the wheat
survivor of a million

noosed philosophies
Africa choked
from his acoustics
a dying world on his face
poplar splints
from sea to shining blindness
he was born invisible
with a tornado smile
and Shango can't save him
from these men
who pray to the turbine
and the jet engine
to their cell phones
and their murdered minks
to their satellites
and their news briefs
but he doesn't care

because
he's a street corner, a stoop
a blindfolded blunt
a nuclear bomb
in the middle of Brooklyn
a thunderclap in the womb of death
a black boy
a tranquilized metaphor
the twice-ghettoed
shackled to the midnight
in his hands.

Magnus

Black Magnus
the drum omega
blue-black mutation
of a transfigured Christ
numerical stranger is
etched messiah of
the darker dark
cosmic graffitist
you wear your genocide well
ye sellers of frankincense
and satellites
of walking scars
and nuclear comas
the fast food of history
racing through your square hearts
concoctors of visibility, they
malt liquor slingers
of the concrete noose
dream stealers, chained
to a visionless arithmetic
ain't no future in dead flags
or un-reincarnated sons

Magnus
hollowed through and through
with folded wombs to ponder
asses to classify
thighs to congratulate
and smack
you, ventriloquist
of America's greatest fears
prophet, you could have
be you is
a rebellion waiting
in the lock-jawed biting
of a wired mouth

speak Magnus
tilt your flask
or fall upon your sword
double-crossed or defeated
by the thirteen stripes of amnesia
by the fifty stars of death
Magnus
your silence is uncanny

speak Magnus
dream and see
flail and flash
scream and conjure
let the stars hear you dreaming
pour out your arms
and re-dream this world
retrieve the nightmares
of bullets whistling
our children's names
dream these coffins back to trees
what if, Magnus
what if you were
our last hopes
you, didact
of our prayers?
our stone pilled messiah
three thousand years removed

Magnus
your ancestors
dreamt you flying.

Torres

Have you seen
the president's daughters
with their newly
renovated faces
sipping hollywood
from the beautiful
womb of commerce
is their corporate-sponsored god
guiding your gun tonight
the desert paralyzed
by your silence
Banquo's blood
ignited boy
stained glass, afraid

Torres you are a suit's fool
a gospelled whorehouse
a boulevard of songs excavated
from the howling flesh
of a bluesman
believer
didn't you hear
the nuanced catastrophe
in the president's speech
speech that orphaned
your mother, left her
snapshots of
the Viet Cong wearing
your father's smile
him drugged mechanical
you infected
by the rabies of oil men
beckoned by the blinding
franchise of adolescence
Torres, you are only nineteen
have you ever seen an oil well

where is your heart
is it somewhere in
the Jim-Crowed
South Bronx
in Ponce
in Vieques
in Washington
wandering the halls
of iron and ice

Torres, did the Iraqi women
clutch their purses
the way they clutch their children
like errors on the landscape
how many Iraqi babies
does it take
to fill your gas tank

Torres, when the bullets
kiss you open
will you think
about your mother
the smell of fresh roses
napalmed into your carcass
your legs torn off
under a street sign
you will never understand

Torres, do you dream
do you dream in landmines
do you get flashes
of you, turned inside out
your organs hanging
dark and heavy
covered in CNN
stock quotes and Islam
the magnolia scented palms
of Texas
down the barrel of your soul

Nixon Vietnamed
into your breast bone
dog tag musical of sand
the helicopters like
background singers
the violins weeping

weep, Torres
weep for all the ghosts of history
for every nineteen year old
boy with a gun
from here to Machu Picchu
for every silent poet
for the makers of uniforms
weep for every broken American
glued to the blue light
weep for yourself, Torres
because I can't weep for you
because this poem is not for you
this poem is for your mother.

Sheeple

Sound bite children
they have brainwashed the sun
the next holocaust
is in the screensaver
microchip the cross thread
of history
a Wolfowitzian future
grown from anthrax
and five planes
Machiavellian
Charlemagne
the towers must go

forty thieves with
Texan blood murmurs
star-spangled freeze tag
toe tag
body bag brilliance
blood baths
and nuclear shivers
and Jesus was there
moon-walking on water
911 tied to a tapped phone
was the president listening

white horse
on the white house lawn
Prozac Jerusalem
road map to death trap
plutonium cloud
on a knit skirt
it's a corporate conspiracy
it's a corporate cover up
they're shredding soldiers again
fighting over land
when they can't live forever

there is a Nazi camp
in Dick Cheney's pace-maker
silent, secret, American
Gestapo dressed in
Soviet news reels
the bay of pigs and JFK
was Julius Caesar
so lift the evidence
from Jackie-O's hair-do
and teach the babies
how to run
teach them how to salute
at funerals

because Jimi Hendrix
is in the Congo
transporting drums
back to Brooklyn
the truth will give you
anaphylactic shock
psychics and magnetic fields
under the Pentagon
6000 years
of secret handshakes
hidden in the shape of a building

and Lady Liberty is riding
a red camel
across a sky
dyed coincidental
blood hounds and war planes
in the fine print
and the west is playing
tantric Russian roulette
with Persia Minor
trying to get their hands
on Nebuchadnezzar's tomb
on the blue prints
to a star gate

wrestling space probes
out of a muslim child's dream

pregnant princesses
car crashes
through French tunnels
paparazzi assassins
dipped in queen's milk
the twentieth century
was a metaphor
drowning
in the collapse
of dream collapse
in the suicide of memory
we are the
apocalyptically
lost.

Pretend

Let's pretend
we didn't leave
codes in rivers
in collard greens
in grits
in gumbo
in a parallel universe
hallucinations of Garvey
wrapped
in barbed wire
whispering remedies
in the Harlem of our blood
sweat curdled on leg irons
throat shackles

bleed me a history book
of granulated sugar
and cotton gins
of smoke huts
and crushed spines
of African souls on European pallets
MIT and Harvard can explain
nuclear fission
but they can't explain
the Harlem shake
Atlantic fever

Goree Island gone mad
broke his neck
twelve times
in twelve different places
he's a zodiac sign on Ritalin
a galaxy with a speech impediment
hand-cuffed to a night stick

and most

of our magicians
were murdered
during the middle passage
because most
of our magicians
took their drums
on board
a small caption
in an even smaller room
"for sale, two negroes and a drum"

a drum
that bends space
reorganizes reality
watch time mutate
rock and roll
slave ships
funky dungeons
beat box
break beat
back beat
broken backs

sweating out
tobacco stains
scatting until
our cells divide blue
swing
swing until
our mothers remember
swing until
our children remember
that hip hop
was invented
by white men
in slave quarters

remember
the unreported rapes

the unreported uprisings
remember that
there are star systems
in our spirit
that it is possible
to dream even
when you are dead
there are remnants
of futures
in the conscience
of your blood
tapping visions into wood

we suffered in silence
guitars on fire
fists in the air
we howled and screamed
until our gums bled
burning crosses
and vacant lunch counters
we will return
to them encrypted
like someone
crashed a slave ship
into the pentagon

and disaster comes blind
like nineteen thousand
light years
dressed in red
making promises
to Wall Street
you may find us
in a stock quote
in a raindrop
helicopters
in the flu shot
war planes
in a tear drop

pretend
but remember
we are
ninety percent liquid
and ninety-nine percent space.

Presidents

Theoretical presidents
oil moguls
and military industrialists
making calls
to the black sea
Cuban cigars
bloody
Ben Franklin's throat
slit from ear to shining ear
confederate flags
abandoned skulls and bones
nazi Rumsfeld
Strauss in the popcorn
Reagan playing his part again

Star of David drawn
on Arafat's back
cancer machined
Castro's fall
Russian Coca Cola
Osama smuggling
America back into America

an opium of truth in his eyes
truth in the truth in his lies
snap shots from space
swastika dreams
for the Bible belt
the red states
shaped like Auschwitz
like a nuclear god
with a tsunami prescription

three blind men
shadow boxing
the headlines

fist fighting the TV

John Walker trapped
in Timothy's lunch box
seven starving children
eating landmines
a picture perfect future
a future pictured perfect
a presidential tear
slides down the presidential face
turns the presidential heart
into a presidential waste
how beautiful.

Blind West

Look at The West
entangled in their
formulaic kleptomania
with their nuclear families
assembly line enlightenment
donating their children
to the chopping block
to the mechanical muscle
of madness

infectus Americus
frock of fascism
fabricate a truth for us
pry it, flesh first
from the incubus
of our forgetfulness
lest we remember
that we too are human
that there is
a two year old girl
in Fallujah
a corporation
has just purchased
her ovaries

Wall Street merchants
clutched in the nebris
of international pedophilia
an inevitable date rape
gone right
gentrified Middle East
9th century kickbacks of
religious pornography
a lab rat giving birth
to a nuclear bomb
bitter the blood of Byzantium

chemical news briefs
intoxicate us with trivia
when a civilization dies
who does the autopsy

trivia
we need it
like a spoon of death
pump us full of the chaos
of the American goose step

all hail the Nazi dollar
the village idiot
and his entourage
of kill-men
all church
and god-eyed
circus paint
and method acting
precision killing
and freedom pills
dress rehearsals
and victory gin

we need a tragedy
someone not blinded by
the consumer friendly deaths
of young boys

spin-simple
we ignore the flags
their mothers plant
drape their coffins
in our socially engineered silence
because psychological suicide
has never been this easy.

Flags

I see a sea of folded soldiers
men too brave to cry
men who shamelessly
die for country
with their hands
over their hearts
reciting graves

I see them
breathing the lonely stars
of poverty
their smiles struck down
like bullet wounds
through tambourines
through presidents

we keep killing our children
without their mother's permission
old men sending
young boys off to war
with the dying milk
of this sick patriotism
smeared all over their conscience
what of humanity

men
submerged
in the galloping grease
of this dishonest freedom
this is more
than lambs fat
or genocide
grown men fighting
over who gets to be buried
in the nicer coffins
how many flags will we raise

before we realize
that flags
don't raise children.

Two-Sevenths

Oil spills
the spinal cord
of a miniature half-horse
bent to an exact angle
syringes filled with
poverty
dictators
and broken emptiness
injected into the spines
of third world children
perspiring poison spoons
eating Jesus out
of the pores of the H-bomb
HBO selling tickets
to their lynching

language within language
torture machines by tortured men
five diluted tongues of
experimental blame
paper money
paper god
paper people
got us believing
in ink

how much
is a dollar worth
in gold
or diamonds
how much is it

worth in mothers
or children
translate that to apples
because eventually
apple trees die
which brings up
the question of
Ayatollah
Hussein
Ho Chi Min
busboys
in the basement of the pentagon
serving the poor
to the greedy

they have developed
new sounds
that control dogs
and gods
sifting deliriously through
the dreams of
the collective idiot
cold blue
funeral beautiful
military servicemen
with their pressed on
clay smiles
patches of flesh symbols

bleeding machine guns
scribbled onto the faces
of the newly bombed
out children
holding hands

singing in a deep red
furrowed field
and in the distance
a small white farm house
filled with pigs
with strings attached

raining a toothless
drum stumble
a blood covered century
nestled in a tight
tiny silver music box
Hitler dressed as a napkin
stained with grapes

prima ballerina style
dancing a soft blue hoop
a philosophical dimple of
military acoustics
a blind folded
assembly line
of politicians
puppets and
trolls
with their nice shiny
Harvard brain implants.

910

America
this is going to hurt
like a power outage
during your abortion
hurt like the 666
is now the American flag
hurt like Adolf Hitler
came back as CNN
but now
the Muslims are the Jews
this is going to hurt like
the Holocaust
was an independent film

slavery was a blockbuster
that made billions
for motherfuckers
hurt like America
was a giant gas chamber
but niggers don't burn well

this is going to hurt
like the wolf
ain't coming in sheep's clothing
the wolf is coming as a chain store
selling FUBU on UPN
with a bucket of popcorn chicken
a cross and a crack pipe
doing an info-mercial
on how to spread AIDS
in Africa

this is going to hurt
like pulling a bowling ball
backwards through your dick
hurt like a urinary tract infection

in your tear ducts

don't cry America
this is going to hurt
like the scent of our ancestors'
blood, caked onto
the psyche of
white America
hurt like the memories
locked up in broken bones
like the steel grin of starvation
the blood covered face
in the window
of colonialism

this is going to hurt
like a fuck you note
to the third world
like a 14 year old girl
giving birth to her brother
this is going to hurt
like a pair of Nikes
two sizes too small
crafted from the skull
of a Chinese sweatshop worker

this is going to hurt
like the World Bank
the IMF
the Center for Disease Control
hurt like your third eye
in a glass of white milk
hurt like the metal in your ankh
was mined by oppressed Africans
hurt like
there is more racism
and apartheid
in your engagement diamond
than in all of South Africa

488

this is going to hurt
like Reagan was playing president
hurt like George W. Bush
was also playing president

hurt like the connection
between the opium trade
and the World Trade Center
hurt like being double-crossed
and framed
by hip hop

hurt like
Iraq
Iran
Afghanistan
Algeria
Nicaragua
Nigeria
Liberia
Lebanon
Libya
Jamaica
Grenada
Panama
Palestine
hurt like being double
crossed and framed
by the CIA

this is going to hurt like Osama
bin Laden lives in New Jersey
hurt like Osama bin Laden
was killed in 1997
hurt like 911
Fuck 911
this is going to hurt
like 1492

1555
1619
1776
1865

this is going to hurt like 3/5
hurt like
Japanese concentration camps
on American soil
hurt like
Tuskegee experiments
like small pox
like reservations
like the word *Indian*
like genocide
hurt like
the bullet that killed
Medgar
Malcolm
Kennedy
and King
was fired from
the same vocal cords

this is going to hurt like
Nat Turner was more American
than George Washington
this is going to hurt
like a black man late
for his own lynching

this is going to hurt bad
it's going to hurt good
and ugly and beautiful

but
most of all
it is going to hurt
because that's how karma works

490

America.

I want to have a baby

I want to have a baby
but not a normal baby
I want to have
a Prada baby
a baby by Coco Chanel
eyes by Versace
hair by Pantene Pro-V
Swatch teeth
Windows XP
Intel chip
Celeron processor
not a smart baby
no

I need a baby
with breast implants
a Botox baby
with 22-inch rims
and leather interior
Gatorade blood
Nike swoosh
Red Cross logo
baby I can donate
to charity
not a baby to love
no

I need a baby that's a trend
a baby that comes
with a cash back guarantee
I need a baby with a website
with a CD burner
super-sized with fries on the side
I am talking about
a state of the art baby
a vintage

492

post-modern
digital
voice recognition
quartz movement heart
baby with a retirement plan

I need a baby
with twelve different ring-tones
with call waiting
and text messaging
a glossy
over-priced
over-hyped
made in Indonesia
with slave labor baby

I need a baby
to give me the light
and pass the draw
I need a baby
that's blazing
like hip-hop and R&B
I need a baby
that hangs out with Jay-Z

I need a baby
with a black album
with a white album
with a grey album
a baby
that's not even a baby
I need a baby
I will believe is a baby
because the baby
went platinum
I need a Che Guevara baby
a baby that believes in revolution
no

I need a baby
that believes in nothing
a vegetarian
tofu-eating baby
fat-free
low carb
high fiber baby

I need a baby
with nuclear potential
I need something
anything
I need something
to keep me distracted
something to prevent me
from feeling
other people's pain
something to keep me
believing
that this
is the best
humanity can do
I need a baby
so I don't have to deal
with reality.

Silent town

Gun metal
silent town
eyes blazing
with a lonesome fever
tears of a torn woman
settling in grandpa's war scars
still fresh
from a hundred years
of cornfields in his dreams
men moving mechanical
fattened with stupidity
the ink still wet under their blades
the signatures of merchants
carve their faces
manufacture their hatred
nobody speaks
the uniforms are silent.

A poem for Obama

We have no more earth
for martyrs
no wooden box to hold you
no tears to squander
you hope the way the sky hopes
suited Malcolm-Clay
carrying that smile
like a sacred place
like a lonely anthem

we've seen this smile before
we know this hope
so honest
so noble
so beautiful
we've seen it murdered
stomped out
dimmed
slaughtered in theatres
in open-roofed cars
on ballroom floors
on balconies
in hotel kitchens

Mr. Obama
we have no more earth for martyrs
no wooden box to hold you
no tears to squander
you hope the way the sky hopes
remember Bobby and
John Fitzgerald
with hair like wheat
clumped with blood
why

why this way comes you

when there are men
with hard boiled eyes
and pistoled faces
lying in wait
why save us
at your daughters' expense

Mr. Obama
when they come
promise me
when they come
promise me that you will smile
pray tell them
of your mother's gentle hands
when they come
these nuclear sons
of Reagan

faces stitched with spin
hearts synchronized
to the AP wire
delivering their
unholy propaganda
like a new born plague
same ones who brought us
god in high definition
trying to define you
promise me
you'll tell them
of the blue beaches
of Hawaii
of your grandmother's stories
your grandfather's war scars
your father's
dreams

tell them of your daughters' eyes
so innocent
so vulnerable

like a beautiful truth
tell them something
to soften their faces
to open their heads
for we have no more earth for martyrs
no wooden box to hold you
all we have
are these unkempt poems
these undiluted church songs
and we'll sing them
scream them even
until our lungs explode
until our vision is blurred
blurred because we love you

we love you
Mr. Obama
because like us
you too, are a searcher
a dreamer
and you speak
a truth so eternal
that even if they put
a billion bullet holes through you
they'll only be making space for the light
to shine through
for we have no more earth
for martyrs
no wooden box to hold you.

War

There is
a McDonald's
in Baghdad.

Yesterday

Yesterday
Malcom's bullet wounds
were mailed
to Colin Powell.

Yesterday II

Yesterday
Nat Turner's ashes
were mistaken
for anthrax.

Yesterday III

Yesterday
Garvey's Black Star-Liner
was found
in J. Edgar Hoover's
closet.

Yesterday IV

Yesterday
Robeson was found
in the Oval Office
tapping out the constitution
in code.

Yesterday V

Yesterday
Harriet's musket
was found
in Condoleezza's bed.

Tele-vision

Middle passage billboard
the blood commerce
of churches
continents hung from
bullet trees
colonialism tight
around the testicles
like 27 years Angola bled
black mothers
with erasers
to their babies faces

husbands
mined like diamonds
Hiroshima fever
yellow Chernobyl
high like powdered history
witch doctor
spin doctor
windmill of sorcery
one arm Russian spy
Soviet classroom
Cuban missile crisis
Ethiopians starving
from sunshine
from freedom
democracy
and pop music

communist Kennedy
bullet wound
the size of Vietnam
razor wire
drawn through
the feeble mouths
of newly minted babies

stretched hollow
with propaganda
the lonely tumored eyes
of future fools
a walking autopsy of spirits
the gun making circus of clarity
of blue confusion

agent orange choke hold
handshake
coke smile
nations fall because of this
new opium shaped warships
politicians at war memorials
stitched to lies
their tears lay naked
in secret meetings
with swords and whispers

don't look back America
the new drug of choice
is fear
and America is so high
I believe I can walk
a cruel striptease of anarchy
of coups
of treason
of lying presidents
premiers
and prime ministers

the roost has finally
come home to chicken
blackened by asbestos
the beheaded dreams
of bleached hearts
the perfect taxation
of patriarchy
can you hear the insipid howling

of Wall Street merchants
the lonely parade
of empty men
the multi-national
side step of reality

watch them dance
the way they shape-shift
metal suits of sorrow
plenty the coffins
we pray for

this isn't sky
this is illusion
so pretend this prayer
for me please
for king George is back
the German fuehrer is back
with maps of stolen shoe shines
cotton field flings
sambo me gentle
slave cough me death
until I go blind
for Washington is diseased.

Bleed

Bleed a silvered wing
cotton ball throats
that either sing or run
or get murdered
like skulls
or cane stalks

men on blue horses
a cold white killing
blowing through their hair
no way back to death
so we stand and watch
spirits under bearded trees
souls burnt down
to soot and song

like rows of sweet
wooden cabins
stolen wombs
of woven women
stretched from
seven foot kettles

liquid ovens
of black survival
left for dead
crying mills
industrial Cinderella
dark like rivers
Africa black
we sing stone oak
and pray Shango comes
spitting the voodoo climax
of change in the wind
to purge the land
to wash their eyes open

history
getting off ships
plantations babbling
a crude drumming

the bend of stairs
the big house
the small shack
the tears in chains
hands chopped off
still clapping at night
to sweat a sound
and pray their gods kill them
before we do.

Workshop

A circle
of turning minds
whispers
water and melodies
a silver delight
dreams and promises
bursting unholy, a fever
braided into the flesh of speech

giant universe
buckets of prayers
logic magic
scribbled smiles
realities evaporating
gem-eyed and silent
time splits
yesterday and Jupiter

talking paper
tell me stories
of a mouse
trapped in a piano
of lights and strings
and pipelines from planets
in your head
turning your veins
into sheet music

walk the Ghandi
with perfect timing
water whisper
a telephone smile
radio dream yourself back to life
in a circle
of turning minds.

Climax

Our climax
will be in the form
of time machines
the gentle breath
of a damp galaxy dancing
dipped in wet woman motions
warm, sweltering
flesh cravings
nimble church girl fingers
slowly spreading
thick liquid darkness
with soft gyrating touches
tearing into the deep
flickering maroon
of your forever space
dripping spirit splitting juices

grasp me
like a weeping
algebraic expression
dying in the pulsating scat
of your schizophrenic
sex grease
hot
sticky
feverish
internal sweat parable
pelvic slave revolt
orgasmic rebellion
let me see
and feel, and taste

the sweet oily spasms
of your vaginal heartbeat jumping
the humid ecstacy grips
of your liquid freedom sighs
I wanna dive head first
into the synapse
of your nerve endings
move for me woman
sneak me into the language
of your salty nipples panting

position your tender
create that divine arc
that religious dip in your spine
so I can touch your Bermuda
with that unpredictable
Jamacian-Al-Qaeda stroke
that will leave your spinal cord
in your forearm

holy water
drink me slow
like god, like heat
call me Jesus of Nazareth
no, call me Judas Iscariot
and lie to me
tell me you feel me
in your wisdom teeth
in your grandmother's dentures
in your soul's ovaries
in your bone marrow
in the prescription in your glasses

let's make love

until we switch species
I'm talking vicious and hard
like molecular physics
like two stars colliding
like the death of a universe
I need neither promise nor illusion
just the quivering anxiety of angels
the strange stir of a brilliant tornado
twisting
turning
bending
screaming
pushing into
the moist muscular flame
of your tightened nebula

here is the code to my genetics
make of me what you please
but please
perspire me an explanation
to why we are here
paint me a make believe
reincarnation

show me how to tease
the tender switch of your miracle
how to lick your scars
until they turn into dreams
press tight against me
like the moment
between two milliseconds
place your petals on my womb
kiss me as if I'm dying
in the aching screams

of your earthquake blooming

let me drink
the fluid from your
spinal column
collapse
grasp
push
hold
hold
your breath
breathe me sweet
tell me you've seen me
in old photos
in dusted memories
in distant cities
tell me you know
who I am.

As sure as

Not sure if there is a god
not sure if I am alive
only centuries communicating
in this surreal curl of existence
this subtle whimpering
of bones surrendering light
like ecstatic eyelids laughing
the death of dreams

the eclipse of veins
penetrating needles
under the seductive grasp
of sexual oil strangling motions
electric pulse
of breath falling faithless
magnetic staggering
of a frantic spirited tongue
beating back and forth
feverishly exhaling steel

trembling lip lung emotions
blue-red naked
smoke-filled tunnels
of screams and demons
pausing

a barefooted twirl
of blood and saliva
bleeding a weeping Jesus
like broken slices of a blue dove
cooing a collapsed April
not sure if any of this is real
not sure if today is Saturday
or 1964
but I know that
the music that moves you

is beautiful.

Sweet woman

How slippery is your soul
can I touch it
and if I did
would it turn me to stone
would I be mesmerized
by its magic
charmed by its
deep shivering spirals
if I should slowly
slip my fingers through
the thick moist silky sap
of your sweetened center

glide emotions through
fields of folded flesh
and feel the heat
of your naked rapture
the arch of your spine
the soft of your ass
in the palm of my hand
slowly
pressing with sweet patience
suffocating in the echoes
of your moans
like a love song with no words
like an orgasm played on a violin
would you flinch or blush
or both

what does it feel like
the sound of your flesh

the thought, that is
does it constantly throb
and dance a circular coil
curled like a slippery seduction
screaming to be released.

Slow

Pull me slowly
into the madness of your lap
into your fevered
love song slippery
flesh miracle unclasping

sweet tangled dark watery
insides dreaming plutonium
to lick gospels
from the melody of your thighs
curling moan movements
silent spread of flesh
shivering pearl pulse

flesh tender as forever
apocalypsing limbs
intertwined like brainwaves
soaked in lust
suck me into the madness
of your lap like a sunset
whispered pelvis
like a blind musician
with a muted horn

in an opium den
the liquid sliding
down the needle
slow spoon of you
bubbling to the bursting
to shoot you vein wise

Mississippi blue song
juices expanding
this ain't love
this is a beautiful suicide
let me rewrite you

pass my tongue
through your arteries
dip a deep dark red cherry
in kryptonite and pass it
so gently across your ass
that you explode into
negro spirituals

I would love to rewrite you
on the stem of tomorrow
catch the flesh
nestled in the sweet
of your visible
close your eyes and love me
linguistic blindfold
elephant feathers
dipped in honey and crumpled
angels

love me
Kansas City black magic
New Orleans gumbo
negroid voodoo
bass drum rim-shot
skin stretched
until the mahogany stutters braille
love me
15 frequencies below insanity
30 frames per second
turn me to dynamite
we'll become stardust together
love me 3.1415926535897

love me until
the humming birds
come covered in
chocolate hallelujahs
love me
in scat

in sign language
in mandarin
in footsteps
in braille
love me cubed root
cotton gin
moonshine pie chart
crop circle erotic
love me as if you found
me inside gods g-spot
stealing moons from heaven
until your insides whisper
the Pythagorean theorem
and sweaty crotch music
into moments of me

taste the audible apostrophe
surrendering the pirouette
of an almost moan
on the cusp of your yearning
hush and press
all that rebellion
back against me until the strings
bend and burst and vibrate
and shake franticly
until we turn the dark inside out
and we both explode into songs.

Strip club

She's a wish surrendering
a cello
viola beautiful
scriptures tickled
in her whole note
liquid spirits
migrating up her
uncoiling
historical spasms
in her sweaty

she could have been
something else
a sandstone figurine
cut from wind and smoke
flesh doves moving
across her abdomen
forgive me invisible
cathedral aflame
star clusters in her lip gloss
she stirs a blue
lap dance sorcery
memories in her dark
woman-soft
seduction poemed
in her sweet infinity
spilling spells

a riddled flame
in her crotch
juju beads
voodoo lips
sex magic woman
possessed by
a silent symphony
Ife in the hip of you

liquid medusa

make me a telepath
point me to the stars
nipples like smoke rings
around the sun
you are Mississippi
and Kinshasa
sheet music and gravity
the equator torn in half
rat traps going off
in your dreams
mule dance aborted
in this dark dirge
like a firm black jazz

gypsy eyes
can I touch you in analog
press parabolas
into your pandora
and dance you slow
on a midnight wind
and whisper
a million
silver-winged butterflies
into your binary code
speak tongues into your belly
translate you from flesh to Kiswahili
from woman to hallelujah
spread you out beautiful
like an earthquake beneath
a waterfall
I'll take you down
way down below time
and touch you so deep
your atoms
will need to catch their breath

so deep

the spirit of your clit
will moan djembes
through the dreams
of swans and elephants
in psychedelic face paint
exploding through lavender moons

I'm talking
flesh frequencies
and psychosexual landslides
and brain bending luminosities

we'll need a fan
a sound proof room
five cubes of ice
a sprinkle of salt
a table spoon of honey
and a fist full of sky
just squeeze
god into these sheets
because in two seconds
I'll move in you so gently
your conscience will shift
1/8 of a nano-meter
open you up so wide
I could time travel
through your pores
and lie naked
in the juices of your genome
memorize your shivers
and leave fingerprints
on your electrons

give you a burst
of passion so warm
and terrifyingly beautiful
that the echoes of your orgasm
will change the pH balance
of the universe

messiah woman
inject me
with the twilight
of your insanity
teeth a sunset
into my flesh
babble a lullaby
into my spirit
pull centuries
through me
because I too
am desperate
and alone
and I'm going to Brooklyn
and I need someone to touch
someone to feel
to know that
I too, I'm for real.